MY LIFE & ESCAPE

HOW I ESCAPED THE CAPTIVITY & SUFFERING OF THE VA PRISON OF DRUGS

BY **MICHAEL ANTHONY MELICE**

ISBN #: 978-1-7321067-1-0

DEDICATION

I want to dedicate this book to my mother, Angela Marie Donatis Manzi, who not only gave me life but helped to shape who I am today. Thankfully, I received from her a strong will, a confident spirit, a loving heart, compassion, and a concern for others. Thanks, Mom: You were definitely one of a kind! I will never in my life ever meet anyone like my mother again, and I am so very blessed for having had her apart of my life. Thanking my Lord and Savior Jesus Christ for having given me the perfect mother. I could not say enough about the blessing that I have always called "Mom." My Mother Angela always wanted the best for family and friends. Sadly, she died on August 8, 2011. I happened to be visiting her before she died, and I knew it would be the last time I would see her. It truly devastated me, as well as family and friends, when we heard this Awful News. She died from cancer at the early age of sixty-nine and a half years old. None of us ever will be the same without her in our lives! This book is written because of who you were, Mom, and what I have become. Thanks Mom: You were the BEST Mother I could have ever been given.

My mother was courageous in her "Battle against Cancer." Why? She refused chemotherapy.

The Cancer INDUSTRY is so GREEDY in their WANT for money that they would rather see millions die of cancer instead of curing anyone! Ozone (Oxygen Therapy) and food-grade hydrogen peroxide will KILL CANCER!! Did you hear this? It's a FACT! But there are too many people out there brainwashed NOT to believe this TRUTH!!!!!

AUTHOR'S FORWARD

Life matters. You matter. I matter. God created us to matter to the world around us in giving purpose to lost mankind. Due to the circumstances of my life, I believe that sharing my life story has a purpose to the silent minority of veterans in the world who may have experienced similar events in their lives and to discover how to overcome them.

So, I share my nineteen-year prison cell (what I call having gone from being considered "mentally ill" from the VA, which is an oxymoron, to being free of such an awful label or any such label). Many of these veterans who may need some help, or even the encouragement in "getting out" of the system that has kept their heart and mind in bondage over the years through the VA Drug program.

This drug program kept my mind in the dark between 1986 and 2005. It's happens in mainstream medicine as well! There seems to be a "pill" for whatever ails you!?!

It's truly one of society's greatest frauds ever perpetrated on the American people! It's wrong, appalling, and highly insensitive to the "Real Needs" of Americans everywhere! Too many Americans have been lied to in regard to so many things, but your health is your wealth. Without your health, nothing else in this life is worth as much at all! I say without one's health: Life is a very Difficult Road to Travel!

Say Yes to Life, continue to be who God made YOU! I am a work in progress that continues to keep on pressing forward! Be the soldier God made you to be, my dear fellow veterans.

Life is a gift. Too many times we live our life as if it were a chore. Realize the Lord Jesus Christ has given to us not only His life, but the gift of everlasting life to those who believe his Good News! *(see 1 Corinthians 15:1-4 King James Version Holy Bible)*

The more you love yourself, the more you can love others. Be yourself. You are unique. Embrace who you are and allow the world to see YOU. Humor, laughter, and joy: There should be more in this world. There would be fewer people in prisons and hospitals.

Though the World Wide Web, known as the internet, is used for bad, it also is used for good in connecting all of us around the world. I believe we have all struggled in this life, and when you see others in the world (on the internet) also struggling, you realize you are not alone.

"Brethren, I count not myself to have apprehended: but this one thing I do, forgetting those things which are behind, and reaching forth unto those things which are before."
                                        (Philippians 3:13)

"I press toward the mark for the prize of the high calling of God in Christ Jesus."
                                        (Philippians 3:14)

"This I say therefore, and testify in the Lord, that ye henceforth walk not as other Gentiles walk, in the vanity of their mind."
                                        (Ephesians 4:17)

It's time mankind wakes up to the lies they have been fed and sees the truth! This is easier said than done. Nonetheless, it needs to be done. Nothing worthwhile in this life is easy.

God created us for His purpose and pleasure. But all of us who are here and have ever lived on this Earth have a story to tell. Isn't it time you told your story? After having lived on this Earth for half a century, I thought it was time to tell my story. So here I am, World … ready or not!

Here is some of my story …

CONTENTS

3 REASONS I AM WRITING THIS BOOK

My hope in writing this book is threefold.

First, I am writing it to tell the truth about my life from my point of view.

Secondly, I am writing this book to share the biblical truth that helped to free me from the spiritual bondage of sin and to liberate my soul unto eternal life! In other words, to share how anyone can obtain everlasting life with Jesus Christ for all eternity.

And thirdly, and lastly, I am writing this story to help veterans realize that they do not have to be medicated with drugs for the rest of their lives. There is a way to break free from medication that the Veteran Administration doctors have provided. I am living proof. I believe it is possible for the majority of men and women in the world to live without drugs, if they choose this decision.

For too much of our lives we Look all around us for the answers to Life. The important answers to this life are found in the Word of God. Jesus Christ created us, the Universe, and his words give us the answers that we all need. There's a difference between need and want.

I once created the quote: "Most folks WANT what they don't NEED; and NEED what they don't WANT?!"

Three Basic Needs in this Life:

1. Food
2. Clothes
3. Shelter

<u>LOVE</u> would be the glue that holds it all Together!

CHAPTER 1

Why am I telling you my story? I confess we all have a story that needs to be told. I only wish that others (my grandparents and mother) in my intermediate family would have told their story while they were alive. It would have been nice to know more about my mother and grandparents.

I wanted to be able to voice what truly happened to me so that my life would be viewed in the perception of how I saw it happen as it happened, and when it happened to me. This way, others could finally know what really truly happened to me! I would hope, too, that others reading my story will also want to share their story. We are all connected, and what each of us does affects others around us. Like a ripple in water, my life affects others around me.

I consider that, despite the trials and tribulations that I have experienced in my life, I am rare and different from most. I'm a winner in my mind, no matter what others may think, do, or say about me.

Everyone will have their opinions and thoughts, but I cannot change what anyone thinks. "To each his own," my mother would say. I am a believer in Jesus Christ, Creator, and Sustainer of All Life!

> *"As unknown, and yet well known; as dying, and, behold, we live; as chastened, and not killed."*
>
> ### (2 Corinthians 6:9)

When this life is over, and the Heavens and the Earth become new, **the only thing that will matter** is whether you are IN CHRIST or IN ADAM! I pray that by the time all who read my book are done, they will be able to say that they are "in Christ," a member of the Body of Christ, whose soul will be eternally in the heavenly places with our Lord and Savior Jesus Christ!

> *"For the body is not one member, but many."*
>
> ### (1 Corinthians 12:14)

> *"For as the body is one, and hath many members, and all the members of that one body, being many, are one body: so also is Christ."*
>
> ### (1 Corinthians 12:12)

We all have to make our own choices on how we live our lives, but the hardest part is living with those choices we make.

I was born Michael Anthony Melice on October 21, 1967 (known as "The Summer of Love"), to Dominick Samuel Melice and Angela Marie (Donatis) at St. Joseph's Hospital in Syracuse, New York. I believe I have one of the greatest first and middle names ever to be given. It has such a wonderful ring to it. My name literally means: "Who is Like God, Worthy of Praise!"

My mother told me that she named me after a character on *The Millionaire,* a TV show from the mid-fifties. Each week the messenger, Michael Anthony, would give a million dollars to some lucky soul on behalf of his boss, a very wealthy tycoon. I am told that the character of Michael Anthony was quite distinguished, handsome, and debonair.

My father told me he met my mother at a bar. They had their wedding banquet at some hall on July 20, 1963, on Spencer Street in Syracuse, New York. My sister Melissa was born in spring 1965. I may never really get the details from my father about their wedding, but photos and video I have seen indicate it was a beautiful celebration.

This was the first marriage for both my mother and father. My father had three siblings who were already married, I believe. My mother had only a brother, my Uncle Richard, who never married. My mother was married once more in her life, and also divorced, well before she died. My father never remarried again, but for thirty years he lived with a girlfriend, Judy, in what you might call a "common- law" marriage.

My father, Dominick Samuel Melice, was a Sicilian man working for General Motors in the Fisher Body Department when my parents met. He cut steel for the trucks of that era: late sixties and the seventies. I don't know very much about my father's parents, but they were born in Italy. I know that my father's mother was born in Siracusa, Sicily, in Italy. His father probably grew up near his mother in Italy. I really don't know.

He said that his father, Nunzio, sold produce at some local market, I believe in the Valley Forge area of

Pennsylvania. I know also that my dad liked to dip Italian toast into his coffee as a child; but then again, who didn't?! His stepfather, a cobbler by trade, had the last name Procoppio.

Part of my father's family sold everything they had and went on the road giving out the Gospel! This is the side of my family where I get most of the Protestant Principles of Faith that I believe.

My father once told me that he wanted to bring my mother to the wilderness and raise a family there. I think we would have all been better off!? Imagine surviving in the wilderness! I could have survived anywhere after living in the wilderness.

My mother was a city girl, and there was no way she was going to live in the wilderness. Her side of the family was from the region of Reggio Calabria, Italy. I don't believe my mother even liked camping?! I believe that fact is really too bad, because it would have been quite the adventure growing up in the wild.

In the late seventies, when the movie *The Wilderness Family* came to theaters, my father took my sister Melissa and me to see it. It is without a doubt one of my favorite movies from the 1970s' era. It's definitely a great family movie with wholesome family values without the violence and sex so many movies bombard you with today!

Just like the movie, *"The Wilderness Family"* a couple named Helen & Scott Nearing who lived off the land in Maine much of their lives, were living similar to the family in the movie! What I read about this couple is that they were probably one of the first pioneering couples in America to be self sufficient.

I had seen the last home they built in Maine back in the late nineties when I lived there. My first ex-wife, Maria Dee Roberts, had a friend who lived across the street from the Nearings' home. One day while we were visiting her friend, I snuck over to the stone wall and looked over at the handmade stone house. The Nearings wrote about their life in a book titled *Living the Good Life.* I was seeing a part of living history, and to me that was fascinating.

Though many Americans today could most likely not make it on their own in the wilderness, I think the thought of living this way is not only healthier, but better for the land and communities around America! But I digress...

One reason why I enjoyed the movie so much is because my father was himself a lover of nature. His love of nature helped me to appreciate the same for outdoor life! I loved fishing and being outdoors. I would relish every moment I had growing up to be in God's living room! This is WHY I thoroughly enjoyed *The Wilderness Family* for that way of life appealed to me very much.

CHAPTER 2

When I was growing up in the first house I lived in, on Cleveland Boulevard in Syracuse, my father had a garden in the backyard, about fifty feet from the back of the house, where he grew corn, green peppers, zucchini, tomatoes, and cucumbers. There also was a round, four-foot-above-ground pool in front of which he built a good-size deck that we could jump off of and sit on. We had a small round table and a few chairs on the deck.

We also had a little patio with some picnic tables where we had barbecues with family and friends. Those were some very good times for my family and me. Like Archie and Edith Bunker used to sing on television, "Those Were the Days...."

Looking back on my entire life, those first eight years before my parents divorced were some of the best times in my life. (Do you remember the phrase "Aren't we lucky we got 'em, good times" from the TV show *Good Times*?) That time period of wonder, discovery, and contentment where the father worked and the mother raised us children and took care of the home is not only over, but it will probably never be duplicated again except in Amish, Mennonite, or other off-grid families.

The world has not changed totally for the better, except maybe in some convenient technology that helps us with doing some things quicker or easier. Relationships were formed slowly, on the phone, in person, or through letters in the mail, all of which rarely happens anymore. The environment around us and our culture has changed for the worse, I believe. But this does not mean that we as a people can't be better to those around us, our environment, or our country.

We definitely have more conveniences, such as this computer on which I am typing this story, or the printer that will print copies of it. The phones most of us have now are cell phones that are basically like a mini computer in the palm of your hand. We have become attached to them like Linus' blanket from the Charlie Brown comic strip.

I recall my father also drove snowmobiles in the backyard, which had hills, valleys, and quite a forest of trees, bushes, marshes, and creeks. This was as close to living in the wilderness as we would ever have in our short lives together as a family.

My mother, Angela Marie (Donatis) Manzi, had worked first (I believe) in a garage changing tires, oil changes, and pumping gas.

She had also had a job working for the Pocket Book Factory in downtown Syracuse. My grandmother, Angeline Gugliano (Mom's mother), and her sister, my Aunt Rosie Terrinoni, along with my Uncle Richard, had worked at this factory with my mother also. I also think maybe another sister of my Grandma Gugliano may have worked with them too.

Which bar my parents had met in, I also don't know; but I am going to believe it was Love at first sight. My mother was a beautiful woman who had a smile that could light up an entire room. My mother, I believe, was such "a catch" that if I had been alive around that time I would have gladly asked her out! I told her that once when I was younger, and she smiled. She always was the life of the party. My father had one older brother, Joe (he was married twice); one older sister, Dolly; and one younger sister, Theresa. He was born in Bridgeport, Pennsylvania, and grew up in the Valley Forge area. His father's first name was Nunzio and his mother's first name was Palma.

My father once told me that our last name was originally spelled "Milice," which means "militia" in French. I looked it up online and found that my grandfather used the name Nunzio Milice on his military draft card. My father said his dad had changed the spelling to "Melice." He Americanized it to get a job. Many foreigners who came to America around the turn of the 20th century no doubt did the same thing to get a job. My grandmother's (Mother's Mom) maiden name was Logan, originally Logano!

When we were growing up, we used to call my father's mother Grandma Procoppio. When she was little (at what age I do not know), she came to America on "The Boat," as she always told us. Tons of foreign immigrants arrived on ships legally. They didn't sneak over any borders. Back in those days, folks came here because they wanted to be a part of this Great Country! They also learned the language.

I believe anyone who wants to live here should learn the language in five years or leave. Imagine how many fewer foreigners we would have.

My Grandma Procoppio first arrived in Pennsylvania. I think her first husband was young when he died, but I'm not sure.

Her second husband was my step-Grandpa Procoppio. He was a cobbler who invented a device called "The Brannock's Device." The story goes that his partner stole the idea from him, and the rest is history.

I've come up with a few inventions myself that I simply did not have the money or know how on how to carry the idea to market. My two ideas were: 1). A vending machine that only serves organic fruits and natural snacks and drinks; and 2). A whole phone on a headset.

One of the few companies I had called about the headset phone was Panasonic. Fifteen years after I had shared my idea with them, a friend of mine in Maine, Beverly Pratt, sent me a clipping from a Panasonic catalog selling my invention. I gave them the idea, but it would have been nice to have my name attached to it.

The song "True North" by Christian singer Twila Paris was partially mine. She added more words and music and changed the title, which originally was "Goin' Northbound." I gave it to her after a concert I saw while living in Maine in 1986.

My brother Christopher also had some ideas that never made it to market. On one of them was for a utility knife, and he asked me if I wanted to invest in his idea and prototype. I didn't have the money to help him invest in his idea. Sadly, if my brother had managed to get his knife on the market, I think it would have sold very well.

Frankly, with the knowledge and know-how that my brother has, he no doubt could have been a millionaire before he was forty. But his lifestyle may keep him from ever becoming one. I once had chased the idea of becoming a millionaire too, but realized I didn't want it bad enough.

I think someone who builds their own home, raises their own crops, and sells what they make to survive are happier than those who make lots of money and live a lifestyle beyond their means because of what the greed for this goal does to them! Life is NOT about things, but about PEOPLE! People are the important part of this life that I feel many have forgotten!

I also once knew the man who created "roller blades." His name was Charles Small and he lived in Charlestown, Indiana. His father's barn door came off one day, and he turned to some men and said, "Well, ya know, if you placed three or four of these rollers under a shoe, I bet you could go really fast!" One of the men standing there stole his idea. He said that if he would have gotten credit for them and made the millions for his invention, he believes he would have not become a Christian?!! The reason Charles thought this is because he would have gotten caught up in the love of money which Holy Scripture tells us is the root of all evil.

So, for Charles Small, the real inventor of "roller blades," becoming a believer in Jesus Christ as Savior was in the long run more important than money. Losing your soul to gain the whole world isn't a good idea, no matter how many zeros you could put behind your net worth. You only have one life that soon will pass; only what's done for Christ Jesus will truly last.

This real-life mini story may be the only place in any book in history that this true historical fact may be found. It was something that Charles Small told me after speaking with him on the phone for almost two years. I met him from a list of Grace Believers I had gotten from Brother Gary Ingison who taught me the doctrine of Right Division in the Holy Bible.

My father's brother Uncle Joe Melice was married twice. His second wife, Mary, was not easy to be around. This was a known fact about Mary in the family. His first wife, Louise, had two daughters and a son with him, I believe. Louise was a good woman, I believe, and always so sweet to us.

Sadly, I don't know my father's side of the family very well. We always had wonderful adventurous times the week my father would take my sister and I up to see his family. My brother came with us most times, but not every time. I grew up around my mother's side of her family versus only seeing my father's side of his family on vacation a half-dozen times, and a few times as an adult.

My Aunt Theresa (my father's youngest sister) was married to a man named Michael (forget when he died and his age), and they had two boys: Mark and Michael. Mark never married, but he has a live-in girlfriend, and

Michael married and I believe had four children. Sadly, he's divorced now. Aunt Theresa has an in-law apartment attached to Mark's house.

My Aunt Dolly was married to a man named Robert, or Uncle Bob, and they had five children: Doreen, Roberta, Mary Dawn, Bobby, and Charlene. Sadly, Roberta and Charlene have died. Uncle Bob also died, all too young! My Aunt Dolly died on August 29, 2017, leaving behind three of her children, a sister, a brother (my dad), grandchildren, great-grandchildren, and many other relatives. She was a lovely woman who had married, had children, and raised them to be good, God-fearing cousins whom I always enjoyed being around!

My sister and I got the chance during summers growing up as teenagers to see My dad's side of his family in Pennsylvania. I love them all very much, but over the years have not seen as much.

My mother, on the other hand, had one brother: Richard Isadore. My Uncle Richard and Mom were very close. I heard once that Uncle Richard had dated a woman, but after their break-up never went back to dating women.

My Uncle Richard, to my knowledge, has never been exclusively with just one man. He's actually quite the gallivant, runaround tramp, as my grandmother used to say.

My grandmother never said anything but must have known? I love my Uncle Richard, whether he is gay or straight. He was always good to my mother and us children as we were growing up.

My sister Melissa and I always wondered what it would have been like if he would have been straight and married with children. We were always closer to my mother's side than our father's side, and they were always genuinely good-hearted, kind, and wonderfully nice people toward us.

I always felt calm around my father and his side of the family. His side was more mellow and quiet, while my mother's side was more energetic and lively. Thankfully, I received traits of each on both sides. My parents were quite the opposite. My father was quiet and more subdued, and he enjoyed the outdoors very much.

My parents first had my sister Melissa Ann, followed by me, and then my Brother Christopher. There is something important about the order of one's birth.

Usually, the first born is spoiled, the middle child ends up getting most of the work, and the baby usually wants to act like one. Those very traits were very similar to how my sister, brother, and I have acted. Nonetheless, despite their quirks and differences, I love both my siblings. We had a poodle named T.J. (Tony Junior) while growing up. My Uncle Richard, when traveling to Reggio Calabria with his mother, my Grandmother Angeline Gugliano, and a few of his male friends to visit relatives of ours, had picked him up back in the late seventies.

Uncle Richard took a huge, now obsolete video camcorder. You know, the ones that were so large that he had to put a whole VHS tape in it to record his trips to Europe.

Our dog, T. J., was my Snoopy, and I felt a lot like the underdog comic character Charlie Brown. He was no bigger than about fifteen to twenty pounds, black, and simply had the most wonderful personality about him. He loved being chased around the house, and at times I recall doing this with him. Sometimes both my sister and I chased him. Of course, our grandmother would always yell, "Stop that running in the house!"

T.J. only lived to be a little over sixteen human years old, which would be 112 dog years! All that I knew when I came home from the U.S. Army on my very first leave (which means vacation), I found that our dog had died. Later that night I cried, knowing he was gone.

My brother had buried him in the backyard of the Syracuse house where we were living at the time, at 231 Hier Avenue. I only got to see a stone where he was buried. I never did see any last photos of him.

I do have a little bit of video of our dog. I really miss him. You could say I truly loved him more than any other dog I ever had. I think every child should have a dog growing up.

I recall when my brother's daughter Marisa, had their first dog, Boca, around. Sadly, Boca died when Marisa was about four years old. Boca was real protective of her, and it showed. It was adorable to see him with her. Great danes only live to be around eight human years, or fifty-six dog years. I can't recall exactly when my brother and his wife bought their current dog, Allie-girl. She is a hyperallergenic dog that does not shed. My brother is allergic to dogs. I love this dog because she loves the attention that I give to her whenever I am around her. My mother also gave Allie this type of attention, which is why she loved my mother so much.

The other two times I owned a dog was when I was married, both times. My first ex-wife and her daughter ended up having two dogs: Miko and Ladie. Miko was three-fourths wolf and a quarter husky mix dog, and he mainly stayed outdoors. Ladie was a female collie who was much prettier than the celebrity T.V. dog "Lassie."

The last dog that I owned was Mattie, whom I had with my second ex-wife. Mattie-girl was a white Jack Russell with black spots. The first day I met her, I was told that she doesn't get close to anybody; but within five minutes she was in my lap. Animals, I believe, are a good judge of character, and I had proven to her that I was a good man.

These four dogs were all wonderful animals, and I was totally blessed to have had them in my life. Now I have the pleasure of being buddies with pets that are owned by family and friends. It's sort like being a grandparent: all the joy with no responsibility of ownership.

I do miss owning a dog, but it's far easier to simply enjoy other folk's pets instead. Besides, I can't bear to lose another dog in my life! If I ever date or marry again, I would gladly welcome another dog. Honestly, the thought of marriage a third time is just too scary a prospect to me. Two divorces is all the agony I care to deal with in that respect. Only the Lord knows my future outcome in that department. I simply take one day at a time.

CHAPTER 3

The day I was born I am told that my sister Melissa, whom I call Missy, was real excited and couldn't wait to see her baby brother. She no doubt was lonely somewhat. You see, my sister has for the majority of her life really never lived alone.

She and I grew up very close to our first cousin Mary Jo (Logan) Marple. Mary Jo's mother, our Aunt Peggy, was our Uncle Joe Logan's wife. Uncle Joe was one of my grandmother's brothers on my mother's side.

Our cousin, Mary Jo, lived down the street from us while we were living in Fayetteville, New York. She was always around. It had a wonderful fenced-in backyard with a garage and three bedrooms. I was raised the first 8 years of my life in this town from 1967 to 1975.

The basement is where my Aunt Peggy had her hair salon. On the other side of the finished basement, we children hung out in the play area. Years later, Mary Jo cut hair down there as well. She also owned a beauty salon on Brooklea Drive in Fayetteville, New York.

Mary Jo, my Uncle Richard, my cousin Kimi Peconi, and

a few others on my mother's side of the family have all cut hair for a living. Even my sister went to beauty school to cut hair and do manicures.

My Uncle Richard Donatis has been cutting hair longer than I've been alive. He started his hair career in 1964, which means he has been cutting hair over fifty years. That's a long career in one field!

I also thought my Aunt Peggy was a very attractive woman. She once had recorded a song, and I NEVER got to hear this song! I have ALWAYS wanted to hear it, and for years it bothered me that I didn't have the chance. We would beg her to hear it, but always said she would have to find it and never did?!

I did have a cousin Jimmy Sacca (on my mother's side) who was part of the Exclusive Dot Recording Artists group "The Hilltoppers." They were once on "The Ed Sullivan Show" in 1952. Cousin Jimmy died in 2015, which means I could have actually met him. He died near Lexington, Kentucky. I never met Jimmy cause our family wasn't close and had no idea if he was alive.

In 2010, I rode by the city of Lexington while driving with my second ex-wife's son to visit his son there. He was going through a second divorce at the time.

I am not sure how old my cousin Mary Jo was when her parents divorced, but I believe young. Like many of my female cousins, I had a crush on Mary Jo back then, and there was at least one time when I kissed her on the lips while playing house. Kids' stuff. She wasn't the only female cousin I kissed.

Most of my female cousins were simply very good-looking women. Then again, they were Italian! Some of the most beautiful women in the world are Italian. Look at women like actress Monica Bellucci, Sophia Loren, Marisa Tomei, Valeria Golino, Isabella Rossellini, etc.

My mother's side was Calabrais, whose relatives come from Reggio Calabria in the southern part of Italy. Calabrais means "hard headed" in Italian. Sicilians are known for making good sauce and good lovers.

Thankfully, I inherited both of my parent's traits. I can cook both in the kitchen, and in the bedroom!

CHAPTER 4

Thankfully, I grew up in an Italian home where much Love, Respect, Hard Work, Ethics, Kindness, and Compassion were part of my mother's side of the family. They had warm personalities filled with generosity and bigheartedness. Nobody is perfect, and neither was my family, but there was a genuine consideration of others that I was taught to be concerned with in our society.

My mother told us we may not *like* a person, but we shouldn't hate them. "Hate is a strong word," she used to say.

"Hatred stirreth up strifes: but love covereth all sins."
                                        (Proverbs 10:12)

My mother's favorite saying that pops into my head every time I am dealing with others I may not fully understand is the following:

"To Each His Own...," which, of course, you would rephrase today as, "To Each His or Her Own," so you'd be politically correct.

My mother never beat around the bush about things in this life, and I don't feel I have to either. But one doesn't have to be rude about it!

"Whatever ... that solves everything," an old friend of mine (David "Scott" Flanagan) would say often. I suppose you could say "Live and Let Live" as a principle of living around others. Allowing them to live as they do, as long as there is no harm done to others.

Long ago before all the thousands of laws, there was only one law in America: Live and Let Live! As long as you hurt no one, you were free to live where ever and with whomever you like! It was called the Law of the Land! It was before taxes on land and wages, and everything else, it seems.

The whole IRS Tax system is a huge fraud since it's been leashed on the American public. See Aaron Russo's film, "America: Freedom to Fascism."

The sad fact is that Americans have been misled to believe that, for example, the federal income tax is somehow necessary. This tax actually goes to pay for interest that the "Federal" Reserve (which is not a part of the "Federal Government") charges the United States on the printing of paper money. G. Edward Griffin wrote about this in his book, "The Creature from Jekyll Island" explaining the money system.

Why in the world can't the United States just buy some printers of their own and make our own damn paper money? The U.S. Note was issued from 1862 to 1971 first during American Civil War and they were known as greenbacks.

I had only the chance to have lived with both my

parents until I was around eight years old. I think we had a wonderful childhood until "it" happened: My parents' divorce.

Gratefully, my father was not a deadbeat. He paid child support and also picked us up to go to eat, stay over a weekend, and bring us on summer trips to see our cousins. We used to stay with our Uncle Bob and Aunt Dolly. They had one boy (Bobby) and four girls (Doreen, Roberta, Mary Dawn, and Charleen). Always a good time except when I got poison ivy or poison oak five times.

When I was thirteen years old, my sister and I were taken to a horse farm somewhere in Pennsylvania that our "Aunt" Peach used to work at. Aunt Peach (she wasn't a real aunt as she was related by marriage; we just called her this, just like I used to call my godfather Sylvester Durandetti "uncle") asked me in front of everyone if I had hair on my chest. After saying I did, she opened the front of my shirt and reached inside feeling my chest.

My father had cheated on my mother (and us, really) with some woman at General Motors. Instead of remaining for two more years at GM and getting his gold watch and pension, my father quit. He regretted quitting General Motors ever since. He says it was too much for him to stay there when this woman was still working there. I didn't feel sorry for him, but I felt bad for my mother and we children, since we were the real victims.

There were two times my father tried taking his life after my parents' divorce. The first time I recall was when I was visiting my Grandma Procoppio (my dad's mother).

One moment I was in the kitchen, and the next moment I heard a noise out on the front porch: My dad had tried to overdose on sleeping pills. I recall the ambulance coming and his mom a wreck. My mother came over also.

The other time was when he got so drunk he had a head-on collision with another car. The other driver didn't die but was in bad shape. If I am correct, my dad and the other driver were both drunk, which is why they both survived. My dad was depressed after my parents' divorced.

When he was young, my father went to a Dr. Boris for depression. The doctor said that either he could take medicine or work it out on his own. He worked it out on his own instead.

I don't think he was with this woman very long after my parents broke up. And for what did my father get out of this "affair"? He lost a good woman who was my mother; the chance to be a full-time father to his children. He lost a good pension, a gold watch, and a good house, and he broke up our family, causing serious problems in our relationships as well as mental scars that I think all of us children have dealt with in our lives.

My brother never really said too much about that whole period of my parents' divorce, but for a number of years he kept what I thought was a grudge against my dad. He doesn't see it this way, but my father came by his place one day (the mobile home of mine that I had sold to my brother around 1995) and, after leaving, a movie was missing. It was an adult film that had been on top of his TV. My brother at first thought it was my father who had taken it. The crook ended up being my dad's girlfriend's brother, and I let my brother know this fact because an item had gotten stolen from his home.

The ramifications my father caused in our future was like the ripple effect that a drop of water causes in a pond. It will affect both my sister and me until the day we die. As far as how much affect it had on my brother Christopher, I am really unsure. He was only five years old when our parents divorced, and he never really spoke much about it.

Divorce is one of the greatest problems in my generation, and it will always have a devastating effect on everyone it happens to in their lives. In my great- grandparents' day, it was almost unheard of, I believe.

I had heard that at that time, my father had tried unsuccessfully to change my mother's mind by taking her to Pennsylvania to see his family. Knowing my father's side of the family, I don't believe they would have tried to persuade my mother to stay in the marriage, and I am glad she chose not to stay.

I don't feel that my mother would have been happy if she remained in the marriage with my father. There's an old saying, "Once a cheater, always a cheater." I certainly don't blame her! I blame my dad for "not keeping it in his pants!" Which is the phrase he gave me as a teenager for advice. Do as I say and not as I do? Of course, it's easier to give advice than to actually follow one's own.

We had lived in Fayetteville, New York, which was an affluent area. I drove by this old home of mine every year when I made my annual trip to Syracuse, NY. I drove by cause I enjoyed the nostalgic memories of childhood. It looked almost the same on the outside as it had for the forty-plus years since we owned it.

Some years ago, I actually did see the inside of the place. I just knocked on the door, told the person who I was, and asked, "Would you mind if I took a peek to see my first home?"

The owner (a woman at the time) allowed me to see it. She did look at me a little peculiar at first, maybe thinking I was trying to scam her somehow?

The top floor looked the same as best as I could recall, but the basement was totally a mess. It was completely and utterly a disaster downstairs, as someone was filling up doorways with cement in two different places and had tried unsuccessfully to make a few walls.

In fact, some of the work was only half done and never completed. The only thing I could think was, "What good homeowner doesn't fix such an UGLY mess of the previous owner like this if she had been there like twelve-years-plus?" When I left the house, I was feeling disgusted by what happened to my childhood home.

In 2017 when I went to visit (my annual trip since 2001), the color of the house had been changed from the tan it had always been (since 1965) to some bright yellow, which made it look very odd. It was sold to some new owners, who I hope plan to update it.

The area of Fayetteville, Manlius, and Dewitt, New York, was a very affluent place, with some really gorgeous homes and beautifully old architectural buildings.

When my parents divorced, we had to leave Fayetteville and head to the city of Syracuse, something we all dreaded doing. We could not afford to stay there. It was cheaper to live in Syracuse.

My mother even brought my sister Melissa and I to see a psychologist at St. Joseph's Hospital, because we were having such a problematic time with the divorce. While crying in the office, Melissa and I were then asked to draw pictures of how we felt. Most children at that age drew mainly stick drawings, but mine were more elaborate at the age of eight. My sister and I dealt with this situation by crying a lot.

The psychologist that Melissa and I had seen happened to be in the same office I was in ten years later as a young adult, when I came home from the United States Army in 1986 as a veteran. Talk about déjà vu!

I have been drawing since I was two years old and have always considered myself to be an artist. I never felt I could make a living as an artist, though. I took graphic arts at a technical school called B.O.C.E.S. I still continue year after year in creating some artwork.

At the V.A. hospital in Altoona, I attended an Art Group every Tuesday. We weren't instructed on any art techniques, but any veteran who wanted to produce art could attend. The group was run by Dr. P. and a man nicknamed "Sly."

In December 2017, Dr. P left the V.A. and moved to Florida to open his own practice as a psychologist, where he would enjoy better weather and less stress. I quit the Art Group after the first Tuesday in 2018.

There was another person who in the first seven years was somewhat involved in the group, both as a participant and supervisor. Her name was Kim D. at the time, but is now Kim L., which is her current name, her maiden name. A guy named Nick had started the group.

When I had met Kim, she was married, but now sadly divorced. I still speak with her from time to time, and I pray that she finds a good Christian man to be with in her life if she ever chooses to marry again.

Sadly, from the very first time I met her I believed that she would divorce that first husband of hers, due to his unsupportive nature toward her work with us veterans.

CHAPTER 5

During my first eight years in Fayetteville, we had some truly wonderful times together as a family, producing many fond memories. One of life's greatest pleasures is spending time with those you love! While growing up, I had the opportunity of being with both sides of my family. Each side was definitely polar opposite of each other in so many ways. My mother's side of the family lived in the area where I was born and raised in central New York.

As a large Italian family, we used to have yearly picnics picnics at Green Lakes in Liverpool, New York, where we reserved an entire area of the beach. Aunts, uncles, and cousins would drive long distances to get there. Those were great times!

More than once, the picnics were filmed on eight-millimeter rolls of film. I had them transferred from film to VHS tapes at the Syracuse Movie Lab. This lab was located at the corner of Park Street and Hier Avenue in Syracuse. Later I transferred them to DVD in Altoona, Pennsylvania, at the Film Center.

Our family really enjoyed each other. A few fished, while we swam, played games, and ate tons of delicious

Italian food made from scratch. And, of course, there was plenty of conversation throughout the picnic area with aunts, uncles, and cousins.

I would guess that there were between 60 and a 100 folks at our family gatherings! Many relatives could not make it, but those who were there all enjoyed these times!

If there was one trait I inherited from my mother's side it was the gift of gab! I know that my mother, sister, grandmother, my Uncle Richard, nephew and myself have the gift! My brother and father do not.

The father of one of my first cousins, Janey-Lynn Spinks, would sometimes fish in front of us children from the shoreline at the family picnics at Green Lakes, using lures and corn. Of course, nobody ever ate the fish at Green Lakes.

The water was polluted, but how it got that way I believe was due to the local industries that simply dumped toxic waste into it without any regard for the water, land or welfare of the people in our community around it. That's like someone pouring toxins in their own pool. It's right in their own backyard, and they failed to care?

I had always heard that they had never found the bottom of Green Lakes. Whether it was true or not, I will never know. After watching the movie *Jaws*, I started to become bothered if anything touched my feet in these or any bodies of waters.

Also, there were many well-known persons who grew up in the Syracuse area, including Actor Richard Gere; Actor Frank Whaley; the Baldwin Brothers actors; former

NFL players, attorneys, and best-selling author Tim Green; author L. Frank Baum (*The Wizard of Oz* books), etc.

Richard Gere grew up next to my cousins in North Syracuse. My mother used to wait on his parents at Ramada Inn. My Uncle Richard used to for years (don't know if he still does?) cut Mr. Gere's mother's Hair. Actor Frank Whaley actually graduated in 1981 from my high school named Henninger High School. I was a freshman the year he graduated, so I just missed him.

My sister and I were only two years' difference, with her being the older. Growing up, we were always together in photos with her kissing me. She and I got along, but we at times fought like cats and dogs. I think for the most part we had a very good childhood; and I will say, looking back, that my mother was simply an amazing mother like no other I know.

The earliest memory of mine was being two years old in a sandbox and making a city with my Tonka toy trucks; my mother was hanging laundry. I actually recall thinking the word "city" in my head as I used my Tonka trucks to create one. I recall feeling safe as long as my mother was nearby.

When I was attending kindergarten, my mother made for me a little carrying sleeve she designed in the form of a "mouse." The mouse was made of gray felt for the head, plastic eyes glued to face, black felt for the round ears, and whiskers made out of white string.

Under the face she sewed a pocket, with Velcro glued onto the back of the head to close the other side of the face pocket, where I would hold my lunch money. A large pin held it on my shirt. I still have that little mouse my mother made for me.

My sister and I on a weekly basis were over at my grandparents' house. Whether it was getting farm fresh veggies and fruits from our Uncle Spike Logan; eating with my grandparents; or staying over at their house, we always seemed to be there or going there. I really enjoyed being with my grandparents on my mother's side. For more than 15 years, I cut my grandmother's and mother's lawn. Also at times, while living in a trailer park, I cut my Uncle Richard's lawn, as well as mine.

My Grandfather Antonio "Bully" Gugliano was quite an amazing man. He was a super athlete in High School scoring an average twenty points in basketball; a track star; and, before going off to the military, he played semi-professional football where he scored an average of four touchdowns a game.

He was a Navy-Marine Medic during World War II, where he received the Purple Heart, Silver Star, and five Presidential Unit Citations. He also played left field for the U.S. Marines baseball team. His troop raised the American flag at Iwo Jima, which is the famous iconic photo that most anyone who sees the picture knows. He had saved the two men on the left of this iconic photo while in combat and before they raised the flag. In 1955 my grandfather was the U.S. Navy championship boxer in his weight division. My Uncle Spike was at the Downtown Syracuse Farmer's Market on North Salina Street for over 73 years, of which I am proud to say nobody will ever shatter this longevity record.

My great-grandparents on my mother's side had first started going to the Farmer's Market in downtown Syracuse back when folks used a horse and buggy.

The trip from the farm to downtown was a good ten miles. Their farm was in Cicero, New York, located where Heffner's Farm is now standing, I believe.

I do have some home movies of these younger days of mine, including birthdays, holidays, and picnics.

Our father's side of the family had come up at least a few times when we were growing up, and we also visited them where they lived in the Valley Forge area of Pennsylvania. My father brought us as young teenagers to visit his family in Pennsylvania every summer, at least six or seven times. With my mother and my father's mother, we also toured Philadelphia and all its historic buildings and places, including Washington's Headquarters in Valley Forge.

I went to kindergarten at Mott Road Elementary School off of Highbridge Road going toward Manlius, New York. It was actually a lovely elementary school.

Some of the memories I enjoyed from that time I am still fond of today.

I had a crush on my kindergarten teacher, Mrs. Ghoul; and I always thought she was a very good teacher when I looked back some years later.

There was even a time once some years ago, on my annual trip to Syracuse, that I was driving around the Fayetteville neighborhood where I grew up and I spotted her in front of her home. I obviously stopped and spoke to her about her life after kindergarten.

I even told her that I had a crush on her back in those early days of my life. Her husband was standing next to her, and she looked at him and then at myself smiling and said, "Oh, I think I knew that back in those days, Michael! You were a very good student, and also the most well-behaved pupil that I had back then as well!"

I felt proud of what she said. I was for the most part one of the most well-behaved people I knew growing up. I was more mature than most my age. I have been mature I believe since I was eight years old. The reason I say this age is due to my parents' divorce.

I always looked to please others around me. Not because I had to, but because I was brought up to be a good man and I wanted to be good toward others. Some folks might call me a people pleaser, but frankly, that's not it wholeheartedly.

I truly love to help others, period. There's no hidden reason. I do it simply because I want to see others happy and blessed. Sadly, in today's society, many folks think there is some ulterior motive when you want to give them something for nothing, or simply go out of your way to be good to them. Our culture today has made it difficult for others to trust you or you to trust others! Just think of the Elvis Presley song, "Suspicious Minds."

There were two little girl classmates in my kindergarten, Donna and Jennifer, who always sat next me or laid down in the grass with me outside. I recall a memory in particular where they took turns kissing me on the grass during recess. Donna had dark hair while Jennifer had light brown hair. Donna's hair was short, and Jennifer's hair was long, usually in a ponytail. I recall them both always kind toward me and protective around others. Donna was more outspoken. She would put anyone in their place if they said something mean to me.

Thinking back on that time, I actually enjoyed both of these cute girls. It would be neat to see what ever happened to them.

There was a huge undertaking of the entire Mott Road Elementary on creating a path in the forest behind the school building. It was a nature trail in which many of the students would spread wood chips (made by the school) along this path during lunch time. Sometimes we stayed out longer than usual. For me, it was more time spent kissing Donna and Jennifer!

One of my favorite toys back when I was around the age of five was a car with pedals. It looked like a race car on the outside and had pedals like a bike that propelled it forward with a steering wheel. It seems like it was made out of a strong tin.

They were fun. Felt like as a young boy you were driving a car, but you got some exercise out of it, too. They weren't very practical unless on a flat surface.

My mother was a Brownie leader for a short time. My sister Melissa was in the Brownies, which is a younger level of Girl Scouts. Many times, I went with my mother and sister to these Brownie meetings. Being a boy around all these cute girls certainly didn't bother me!

CHAPTER 6

I had Three good childhood friends on my street. They were Eric Burgin, David Vigliotti, and Teddy Wheeler. David, Eric and I were best friends before inviting Teddy to our "friendship circle."

David, Eric, Teddy, and I were always playing outdoors together. Eric had a huge forest-like place in his backyard, accessed by a path on the left side of his property. That same forest-like place was behind my house, too, beyond my father's garden.

Along the path at Eric's house, raspberries grew on huge, long, and intricate vines. Eric and I would pick them and share them with David's and Teddy's families, as well as our own.

Eric's mother, Sue, was a sweet person who seemed a hippy. I had a crush on her. She always drove a VW bug, and she dressed casually. She wore glasses, too, which is a turn-on for me with women. She had a very gentle personality that made you feel at ease around her. She always helped us clean the berries. Being that we picked them yards away from Eric's front door, we brought them into his house first.

My nephew Dana said once, "Wow, Uncle Mike, who didn't you have a crush on back then?!" Well, I did have a lot of very attractive relatives and family friends growing up around me in central New York!

Eric's mom made raspberry pies with the extra berries we picked. Our favorite thing to do was put them in a bowl with milk and sugar and devour them.

Back in the day when I was growing up, we had a milkman come to the door with milk on a weekly basis.

My mother would leave out empty milk bottles and pick up the new ones when they arrived. My brother Chris was so different than my sister and I that there was a long-standing joke he came from the milkman.

My Mom would make whipped cream from the cream at the top of the milk when it arrived. When she wasn't looking, my sister and I would take a tiny bit on our fingers and eat it. If we got caught taking any, she would yell and slap our hands. Love and discipline are the two main principles in raising children.

Next door to my house on the right side was a German couple with thick accents who could grow a garden like nobody I ever saw back then or since. My dad had a decent garden, but our German neighbor's garden was impeccable!

Years later, I went to knock on the door and see if they still lived there. The wife still had remembered me which, at her age (guessing 92), I thought was amazing. The husband had died some years previous, and it was just the wife and her married daughter who came to the door and spoke to me. Lovely folks! They were always sharing bounty from their garden. My father did, too. Folks back then shared more, I believe.

CHAPTER 7

I think families today are not as close due to the disconnectivity of us all on this planet created by the electrical devices we own. You constantly see folks looking down at their phones and not really enjoying the view in front of them.

One day we were visiting our cousins Kathy and Ed Koehring, related to us on my mother's side. I had a huge crush on their daughter, Dawn.

· Once as a preteen I had the opportunity to kiss my cousin Dawn, and I took it. It was downstairs in the basement of her home in North Syracuse. My sister Melissa and I went there one evening to visit their family with our parents, and we were told to go play with the daughters. Ed and Kathy Koehring had four daughters. I recall my sister and I went downstairs with Dawn.

She was showing us something that her parents had bought her, and all I could think of was how am I going to kiss her.

Finally, my sister went upstairs for some reason, and it was just Dawn and me. I really don't recall how it all happened, but it was a very brief kiss we shared on one of those house-support poles that keeps up the floor. I remember after that kiss, I felt like I was on Cloud 9!

My mother was an amazing and beautiful woman! I once joked with her that had I been her age growing up I would have asked her out. She was beautiful on the inside too. She was truly a people person! She could speak to anyone, anywhere and anytime.

I thankfully picked up this trait from my mother.

She had a way of making others feel comfortable around her. She also did "Live to Give" (copyrighted by myself in 2014), which had been my philosophy most of my life. Though I have cut back some on giving, due to how cold and indifferent the world truly has gotten!

CHAPTER 8

My grandparents (on my mother's side, the Guglianos) had a lovely ranch home at 623 North Avenue in Eastwood, New York. They had friends across the street, Hank, Joanie, and their three daughters (Julie, Valerie, and Donna), who had become close friends of our family from the sixties to the present time. All three daughters actually babysat my siblings and me.

Sadly, Donna has left the area and doesn't contact them at all. No one knows why. Julie and Valerie (I had the biggest crush on Valerie, though they were all attractive girls.) still come around their parents. On occasion when I am in town visiting them, I have seen both Valerie and Julie. Hank and Joanie are real wonderful parents.

My grandparents' house had a huge paved driveway with wagon wheels attached to lamp posts on each side. They had two bathrooms (one in the basement and the other on the main floor); three bedrooms; a front room; a big kitchen; a den; and an enclosed garage where they kept a stereo and refrigerator. In fact, they had three refrigerators: in the basement, garage and kitchen.

There was even on the stairwell going downstairs to the

basement a crawl space that had a door that lifted up with a lock attached. I never liked opening it, and neither did my grandmother. There were a few times I had to crawl in it to get something; it was too dirty and dusty. Kind of a creepy place, too!

Amazingly, I recall one of their refrigerators lasted at least fifty years before they sold it. The person who bought it used it another fifteen to twenty years before it broke. I mention this because I never in my life heard of any appliance lasting sixty-five to seventy years. Have you?

There was something so wonderful about my grandparents' home. Maybe because there was always love, drama, and something new going on in their home. I always felt "at home" when I arrived.

No doubt it was because we were always so close to them throughout our lives. Sadly, I wasn't around when my grandmother was dying (I did speak to her on the phone the night before she died), but I did make the funeral thanks to my father's girlfriend Judy's brother who drove us through a storm from Virgina to NY. There was a huge Nor'easter snowstorm with tons of snow, wind, and plenty of vehicles that simply couldn't get through the roads. We drove back to Syracuse on March 13, 1999, from Alexandria, Virginia: the day my grandmother died.

CHAPTER 9

Well, one evening my sister Melissa and I were over at my grandparents' sleeping on a Friday or Saturday night, when Cousins Peter and Jenny Pecone, along with their daughter, Lisa, came over. Now, Lisa was somewhat of a homely looking young girl, but nonetheless sort of cute in my eyes. I did have a slight crush on her when I was younger.

My sister and I were playing hide and go seek downstairs at that time, when we heard them coming in the home. I had a good hiding spot, and my sister was still looking for one. There was only so much space to hide.

What happened next is totally true. Most would call it molestation, but I did not understand that at the time. I am sure it affected my mind. Lisa was twice my age, which points out that it did affect me in preferring older women from then on in my life.

By the time Lisa slowly, and quietly, came downstairs, my sister had found her hiding spot. My sister always seemed to pick the downstairs bathroom as a hiding place, and I always picked either behind the bar or the big walk-in closet. Everything was quiet except for the conversations I heard upstairs. There was no noise for about five minutes, and my sister never came over to where I was hiding. Thankfully, she never found me that night either.

What was about to happen to me this evening is difficult to realize that it ever took place. My sister Missy was around the age of nine while I was around seven. We were both in our pajamas and slippers and would be asleep right after watching a movie and brushing our teeth.

Sometimes we could ask my grandmother when relatives came over to stay up longer, and we were allowed because of that fact. She would say, "Yeah, oh, alright!" Sometimes she made a little stink, and the cousins would say, "Oh, come on Ang, there's no school tomorrow!?"

Lisa somehow must have known right away where I hid, because, as I was kneeling behind my grandparents' (mother's side) bar in the basement, I suddenly heard her footsteps. Really carefully, I looked up and saw Lisa coming toward me, and then she kneeled down on the floor next to me.

She pressed her pointer finger against her lips as she whispered, "Shhhh...be quiet, Michael." I looked into her eyes, as they were now level with mine, and didn't say a word. I recall a rush of butterflies in my stomach, and then they vanished.

She looked at me and began moving her lips close to mine as she kissed me, slowly and quietly. I can tell you right now, I was real excited about this experience. What is a young man to do?

I wasn't as brave as Joseph in the Bible, who ran away

from Potiphar's wife as she tried to seduce him. I didn't grow up with anyone who would have run away in that moment.

Paul the Apostle instructed Timothy in the book of 2 Timothy:

"Flee also youthful lusts: but follow righteousness, faith, charity, peace, with them that call on the Lord out of a pure heart."

(2 Timothy 2:22)

After kissing me some, I felt her left hand reaching down and slowly pulling my zipper downward. After she had done that, she reached into my underwear and with her right hand took out my member and began massaging it. After she had been stroking me for what seemed like twenty minutes, she suddenly stopped.

I didn't know exactly how wrong it was, but years later when I was living in Maine and explaining this event to a counselor, he said, "You were molested! She could have gone to jail for that!"

I shouted to him, "What? You really think so!? I was seven and a half and she was almost fifteen years old. There was nothing illegal about it?!" It may have been **morally wrong**, but **not illegal**, right?!

After Lisa was done stroking me and placing myself back in my pants, she zipped them up and helped me to get up. She kissed me on the lips, gave me a hug, and said, "Now, don't tell anyone. It's our little secret, alright?!" "Sure," I said.

She hugged me, and I held on longer than usual.

Honestly, I was slightly lightheaded and sort of dazed.

I kept it a secret until about thirty-five years later, when I told my Uncle Richard what happened. Uncle Richard wasn't surprised at all when he had told me, "She blew half of East Syracuse!"

I was really shocked at this statement. Never in a million years would I have ever thought about Lisa Pecone this way. She always was so quiet a person. I kept it secret from my mother a few years longer after telling my uncle.

The whole time this experience went on downstairs, my sister never found me. I had heard her leave the basement and head up to watch television in the den where we watched it with my grandparents.

I think she sounded a little scared and began yelling to my grandmother, "I'm coming up. I can't find Michael!" She used to do that when leaving the basement because she was really creeped out at night by that cellar. It used to give me the creeps, too, during the night. Your mind starts to play tricks on you when it's dark.

I walked away from Lisa and headed upstairs, not knowing exactly how to feel about what happened. I was slightly confused, but it didn't bother me at the time.

Nobody suspected anything after we came upstairs. My grandmother asked me where my sister was, and I told her she was watching TV. My grandmother, Peter, and Jenny were so busy talking they never saw my sister head into the den, which is off the kitchen where many Italians pretty much live in our homes most of the time.

CHAPTER 10

I was probably around ten years old when we lived at 1212 Park Street, in Syracuse, NY. Our neighbor was a cute girl my age named Rhonda Love (don't ya just "love" that last name of hers?!), who lived next door to us. I told her once, "I'll show you mine if you show me yours?!" Well, she said, "Yes!" My sister and I used to play with her and some other children in the neighborhood.

One evening we decided to "Show and Tell" each other's private parts. Well, it was Rhonda, myself, my sister, and about two other little girls who gathered around us. I was hoping it would have been just Rhonda and me. We were in this fenced-in area where Italian purple grapes were being grown between her house and the apartment house where I lived.

I unzipped my pants and pulled out my part. Now, mind you, my sister Melissa, a little blond girl with ponytails, Rhonda, and maybe a few more little girls were all in a circle. Rhonda looked at me and smiled. She was either ten or eleven. Rhonda then unzipped her pants and showed me her private area. We were both very close to each other, facing one another. She touched mine and I touched hers.

We zipped our pants back up and everyone but she and I left the area. I went over to her and kissed her on the lips some. She smiled as she looked into my eyes and said, "Thank you, Michael!" I told her she was welcome, as I did it again. I had been infatuated with Rhonda from Day One. I turned to her and said I would see her tomorrow. She smiled at me and waved good- bye.

One thing that really creeped me out once was finding the "Satanic Bible" in my grandparents' basement after my grandfather had died. My grandmother (knowing I love to read) said that I could go pick out whatever books I wanted. I am not sure what book or books I picked, but I ended up tossing that "Satanic Bible" in the trash! My brother saw me do it.

My brother ran and told my Uncle Richard about it. Uncle Richard told me, "It could be valuable. Now go get it out of the trash and put it back on the shelf." I tried to argue with him, but he told me to go get it. I obeyed. Then, before my brother and I left my grandparents' home, I snuck downstairs and again placed that evil "Satanic Bible" in the trash. I said nothing to anyone for a week.

I recall my brother Chris saying he was going to tell on me. Being the baby of the family, he told my mom. I told my mother that it was pure evil. Of course, my Uncle Richard had found out and yelled at me again. I wonder how long that Evil Book of Lies was in my grandparents' home?

I was actually pretty proud of what I had done! There was no way in hell that I was going to allow that book to remain in my grandma's home.

There was no getting away with anything at my grandmother's home! We were all fairly good at her home. I wanted no part of the punishment, so I chose to be a very well-behaved child most of my youth! I wasn't an angel, but I feel I was better behaved than my siblings. My mother agreed with me on this fact.

My grandmother was married three times. The first man was my real grandfather, John D'Donatis. The second husband was a German named Larry Krier. And the third husband was who we all called our Grandfather Antonio "Bully" Gugliano. My siblings and I grew up always thinking of him as our real grandfather, even if it wasn't by blood.

I had always heard that the first two were abusive toward her. My Aunt Nellie in Chicago once told me that she knew that my Grandfather Antonio really loved her before them all, but did not get the chance until she was divorced from the first two.

Imagine being so sure that a woman was going to be with you, and then have to wait so many years while she was with two other husbands. It always seemed pretty romantic to me and reminded me of Jacob having to wait for his Rachel in the Holy Bible. Jacob waited seven years, but my grandfather probably waited longer.

Grandpa Antonio "Bully" Gugliano also read his Holy Bible and ended up placing money in it before he died. Like he was trying to tell my grandmother to read God's Word? My grandfather slept on the left side of the bed (facing the Bible), while Grandma slept on the right side.

My Grandmother Angeline (God Rest her Soul) would sometimes use her winnings from playing cards on the weekends with friends and relatives to take my sister Melissa and me out to eat on weekends. I don't recall my brother Christopher being with us on those outings very much.

One of our favorite places to eat was Arthur Treacher's Fish & Chips, named after the police officer, Arthur Treacher, in the movie *Mary Poppins*, The last Arthur Treacher's I recall seeing was up in Liverpool, New York, back in 2010, while I was visiting Syracuse. The next year it was gone.

Supposedly there are still a small handful left that have been around since the early seventies. This was news to me when I looked it up online.

CHAPTER 11

My grandmother Angeline Gugliano was an old-fashioned woman who didn't put up with bull crap. I asked her once, "Grandma, what's your middle name?"

"I have no middle name!" she responded.

She was a practical, no-nonsense lady who taught us how to cook (she had amazing cooking skills); clean; do laundry; sew (everyone should know how to sew); play cards (from Go Fish to Gin Rummy. Never understood Poker); respect our elders; play bocce; have good work ethics; and enjoy our Italian family traditions.

We had better never tell her we were bored or we were put to work. She had a great sense of humor and style. God and Family were the two important values that she and our grandfather taught us to respect and enjoy.

When it came to how she would discipline, it was by whatever she had in her hand! I was always a people pleaser it seemed, and never wanted to make her, my grandfather, or parents upset with me enough to punish me!

Of course, my grandma's understanding of God stemmed from the lies the Catholic Church spouted to her.

Later in my life (at the age of twelve), I had left Catholicism behind never to return.

Seven years later in my life I would learn what the Word of God had truly taught! Sadly, the largest denomination in the world are what Pastor Richard Jordan of Chicago, Illinois, refers to as "Ignorant Brethren." Ignorant doesn't mean stupid, but lacking in knowledge.

I later had become a non-denominational Grace Believer. There is no need for a denominational system, and God had stated this in His Word:

"Speak the same thing, and that there be no divisions among you; but that ye be perfectly joined together in the same mind and in the same judgment."
(1 Corinthians 1:10b)

CHAPTER 12

I am proud to say that my family brought bocce (an Italian game) to Syracuse, New York. They started the first and only bocce league I ever knew of there in town.

It seems to me that the only folks who were part of the Syracuse Bocce League were my relatives on my mother's side and some of her friends. It's not around anymore, but they used to have yearly banquets and they gave away trophies. It was simply another place to gather socially.

The park where they played was called McChestney Park, near the corner of Pond Street and Grant Boulevard. This happened to be around the corner from Grant Junior High, which became Grant Middle School the last year I was there. Uncle Joe and Aunt Rose Terrinoni lived across the street from Grant School.

To this day, my Aunt Rosie's son Joe still lives in that house. It's really a wonderful little home. It had a garage, front porch, and I believe three bedrooms. It was very well kept, clean, and always very neat. I used to love going over Uncle Joe and Aunt Rosie's house to visit. Visiting family all my growing up years was a tradition mostly done on the weekends, but occasionally during the week.

One one visit to Uncle Joe and Aunt Rosie's house, a strangely funny thing happened.

First, I want to report sadly that my wonderful Aunt Rose Terrinoni died on April 15, 2017. She was ninety years old and suffered much the last two-plus years of her life. I will always miss her. Her husband, my Uncle Joe, sadly had died some years previously of prostrate cancer.

Those who were there on that visit years ago in my aunt and uncle's home were: my mother, Uncle Richard, my sister Melissa, my brother, myself, their son's Joe and Sam, Joe's son Joey the twin, and I think possibly Chantelle, who is Aunt Rosie's granddaughter.

Well, there we were all congregating in the kitchen, talking and enjoying coffee and sweets. My Uncle Joe had a brown paper bag that my Aunt Rosie got from the bedroom.

He says to everyone as he opens the bag, "Okay, everyone, watch this!" He pulls out a double-sided dildo and we all laughed hysterically as he put it back in the bag. You can just imagine the uproar of laughter that began! Much of my mother's side of the family all had a good sense of humor. This happened around the mid-1980s! I never knew anyone else with a story like this in their family history.

CHAPTER 13

There was a dead-end forest (that extended from the end of the street and out) on Cleveland Boulevard, the street I grew up on in Fayetteville, New York. My friends and I would go down to explore it on a weekly basis. Back then, at the age of eight, that forest was like some huge country to me and my friends. We were told not to go down there very much, though it was definitely safer in my day as a child than it would be today.

If I had a child today, she or he would in no way be wandering down some trail to a small forest where God knows what could be lurking there. Aliens, strange creatures, bears, punks, or pedophiles, oh my! The world today just isn't as safe as it was in the late sixties and early seventies.

My three close friends—David Vigliotti, Eric Burgin, and Teddy Wheeler—and me had some real fun times together. We didn't have a bunch of electronic gadgets to take us away from the great outdoors and beautiful nature! I truly loved being outdoors and exploring. Children today, I will guess, aren't doing this as much.

I lived two doors from Eric and his family, and we were

both a half block away from Teddy and David. Teddy and David lived kitty-corner from each other at the end of the street just yards from the dead-end "forest."

My father and Eric's father, Jim or James Burgin, who happened to be chief of police (and a state trooper before retiring), used to hunt for deer at the dead-end wilderness. I always enjoyed venison meat. God intended for us to eat wild game that isn't processed with hormones and chemical additives.

I remember one time when a guy on a motorcycle landed head first as he flew over the hill down into our dead-end! A bunch of neighbors watched the scene as policemen, firemen and paramedics were there helping this poor guy who flew off his motorbike. Never saw the man again, and I always wondered what happened to him?!

My friend Eric and I dared each other one afternoon to start digging up the first green on the golf course across the street from us. David said no, but he watched us, and then when he heard something (I thought golfers) he ran off.

"That chicken, figures he would run?!!" I said aloud, shaking my head.

Before we knew it, there was a groundskeeper yelling and chasing us from the course.

Despite being grounded, scraping knees, falling, getting into mischief, or any kind of trouble, childhood for me before the age of nine was actually ideal America: sort of a Norman Rockwell painting. The first nine years of a child are the most critical in development of a person is what I have heard, read, and believe.

Growing up in my Italian family for me was one of the greatest times of my Life. Family was important, and stressed from my mother, aunts, uncles, cousins, and especially my grandparents.

What has happened in the second half of my life with our family would have those who have died rolling in their graves. It all started with the death of my grandfather, then my grandmother and mother.

My mother and her mom were two of the most important people in our entire family. When they were around, this family was close, and now at my age of fifty-plus we are scattered like the wind. Geography isn't the only thing that separates us. I have always felt like a loner, and now more than ever.

Even when I visit Syracuse every year, I feel distant to much of my family.

Speaking of Norman Rockwell, my Cousin Shirley, her husband Tony, and her daughter Cindy had grown up around this artist's life in Pittsfield, Massachusetts, same town as him.

My cousin Shirley worked at the local bank that Mr. Rockwell frequented on a monthly basis. He even stopped at her teller window at least once. Being an artist myself, I would have gotten his autograph on any of his work at least once.

Cindy had not known why all these years growing up around this Iconic Artist that her family failed to get his autograph?

CHAPTER 14

I recall one traumatic thing that happened to me as a child, probably when I was five. I got attacked by a large dog. The dog's name was Midnight, and of course it was the color black.

I don't recall what kind of dog, either, but I suppose I had PTSD from that dog attack. For the longest time, dogs bothered me. I think it may have been a short-haired Weimaraner.

I recall another dog incident, where I had to hide in bushes to escape its wrath. I happened to have been in some person's yard when the dog got loose of its collar and started to bark at me. The dog finally got tired and allowed me to run safely away. The dog happened to be a large German shepherd.

One of my favorite classes in elementary school was music. We sang many folk songs back then, because it the late sixties. One of my all-time favorite songs we sang was "The Lion Sleeps Tonight."

Of course, in kindergarten my two favorite things were snack and share time. After snack time was nap time.

I used a white silky blanket back then, similar to Linus' blanket in the comic strip, "The Peanuts Gang," with Charlie Brown. I loved that blanket and took it everywhere just like the Linus did. I even had three porcelain dolls of Lucy, Snoopy as the Red Baron, and Charlie Brown, which sat on shelves in my bedroom as a young child.

For me, school was a great time. My mother used to tell us children, "School's the best time of your lives! You watch: one day you will see I'm right!" And though there were times throughout my school career I may have dreaded at the time, she was correct.

I am sure that my sister Melissa and brother Christopher never felt this way. Of course, they did not graduate the normal way. Melissa got her equivalent GED and Christopher got his GED.

My Uncle Richard and I were the only two in the family to have graduated with a huge ceremony and a party with family and friends afterward. My mother and stepfather Rocco Manzi had made my 1985 Graduation Party a success. I helped put up the tents and tables, as well as take out food and drinks.

I actually used to look forward to going to school because I was a social butterfly and enjoyed learning new things and being around new faces.

You see, I enjoyed not only learning in school and socializing, but when I would get home I loved studying too. Life was my classroom, and I was always reading, writing, and making art. I also used to make model cars and airplanes, too. My mother would help me hang the airplanes from my ceiling when I was done gluing them together.

Melissa used to play with Barbie dolls. Little girls had been doing this since Barbie came out in 1959. Our cousins Shirley and Tony D'Agostino's daughter Cindy lives next to a man whose mother Ruth Handler was responsible for creating the Barbie doll. It's a Small World After All, as Disney might say.

My sister always asked me if I wanted to be Ken when she played. There were some times where I did. We were very close, and I enjoyed being with my sister during those years. It's not that we never fought because we did: like cats and dogs! But I always made it a point to apologize, give her a hug and kiss, and tell her I was very sorry and that I loved her.

When I was about six or seven years young, my mother, sister and I went to a television studio where they aired Saturday matinee movies. Back in those days, there was a TV show called "Salty Sam," in which this nice, older man with glasses was the host.

Well, I was on the "Salty Sam" show with my first neighborhood crush I had—a girl who lived on my street named Susan Nicholson. I used to call her Suzie while Mom called her Suzie Q. The Nicholsons had lived almost across the street from my friend David Vigliotti on my block of Cleveland Boulevard.

On the show, I was in a contest to see who could stack cups and saucers higher than the other person. Well, I rushed to stack mine while Suzie took her time. I recall

MY LIFE & ESCAPE

my mother shouting at me to take my time. Well, she won, of course, because my cups and saucers fell before hers. Maybe subconsciously I let her win because I had a crush on her.

I recall giving her a hug and kiss on the cheek after the contest and she blushed. I recall being caught kissing her as a youngster in her backyard near a tree. The name I got teased with was "Michael-Michael Motorcycle," who kissed all the girls and made them cry. I did visit Susan's mom once as an adult at her home in Fayetteville, which was somewhere across East Genesee Street from what once was called the Fayetteville Mall.

It was a nice visit really, and the sad fact was that Mrs. Nicholson had not seen my family in years. She was so close to my mom back in my childhood. I had told her about my crush on her daughter, Susan, but she knew already. I had grown up in the suburbs and now needed to be able to survive the city streets. The city is really like an asphalt jungle.

Living in the city was a serious adjustment. All the years I grew up in the city truly prepared me to live in the rest of the world! The phrase, "If you could make it here, you could make it anywhere," was something folks in big cities like New York City would often say or sing; but frankly, anytime a person grows up in a big city you learn survival skills.

When I was growing up in the seventies and eighties in Syracuse, there were around 350,000 people living there. One time I think the population of Syracuse was almost

400,000. There are about 130,000 people now, give or take.

During this time period, from 1970 to 1987, it was to me a magical time to grow up, and I am glad I had the opportunity.

My generation could occupy ourselves with something as inanimate an object as a stick. Imagine giving children a stick today and telling them to go outside and have fun! It would be near impossible for most children today to be able to fill their days with just running around outdoors in the bushes and trees exploring and enjoying nature.

It also was a great time of actually talking to neighbors, saying hello to others we did not know. We used a phone on the wall, played records on a record player; used cassette tapes to play music or books; played board games; respected those older than us; watched TV mainly on the weekends or one show at night. By the time we were grown up, you could sing with Don Henley that it was the "End of the Innocence."

CHAPTER 15

A fter my parents' divorce, I grew up on the north side of Syracuse. First, we moved across from Northway, a discount grocery store, at 203 Pond Street.

If you could stand the damaged building and products, then you would find some groceries items. It's where my mother met a woman named Sue Catalano. My mom went from being this quiet woman to a woman who was louder, always on the move. Sue was a good person who was loving, giving, and compassionate. She also was a very loud person who seemed to have a swear word in every sentence she spoke. My sister Melissa used to explain Sue as, "Oh my God, she'd say 'F--- this, and F--- that' whenever she spoke."

"Neither filthiness, nor foolish talking, nor jesting, which are not convenient: but rather giving of thanks."
(Ephesians 5:4)

All it took was a little leaven (sin) injected into our lives through the lifestyle of this woman Sue. I really did love the woman, and I am sure that my brother and sister along with my mother loved her, too. But sadly, it corrupted all of us. I think the moment we left the beautiful suburbs of

Fayetteville and moved to the city of Syracuse, we started going downhill in our lives as far as our way of life.

It was simply going from a cleaner environment where folks were upscale to a dirtier environment where folks were a lower-class status. Frankly, though, lower- class folks are easier be around than the upper-class. Upper-class folks tend to have an attitude like they are better (not always, but generally speaking), while lower- class tend to be more humble, open, and a much better attitude (not always either).

There were some really good folks I met in the city, though. This was simply because of our financial situation now. My father paid child support and used to come around and take us places, out to eat, on vacation, fishing, etc.

I have some very fond memories of those days with family and friends, and the areas I grew up in. Every year, when I head to Syracuse, I always drive through areas I lived and enjoyed. It's always very nostalgic for me.

One of my favorite places is called "The Old Erie Canal." The Erie Canal is a 36-mile canal hand dug by men between 1817 and 1862. It's a nice place, by the waterside path, to reflect on things in one's life. Memories are simply reflections of what used to be. Whenever I visit New York I like to go to this canal and enjoy nature with my thoughts.

CHAPTER 16

My mother's friend Sue had two boys. Teddy was my age, while Tommy my brother Chris' age.

Sue simply showed us "the ropes" of city living, along with being our tour guide. She would tell us where to go, and where not to go shop. She was truly a genuine friend to my mother and we children, and she never beat around the bush with words. She was real practical, another single mother who knew tons of folks to whom she eventually introduced us.

Sue was Polish, and of course the phrase "Pollock" was thrown at her by folks who knew her, but it wasn't overused. I never liked calling anyone any names, because my grandmother, mother, and uncle had taught my brother, sister, and I that it wasn't a nice thing to do! I heard such awful names, including "Dago," "Guinea," and "Whop," insulting my Italian heritage. I was too proud of my heritage to really care, though! Italians have accomplished many wonderful things in our country and the world. No group is perfect though!

The first male friend I met at our first apartment in Syracuse was Frank. Thanks to Frank, I began playing

"Marbles and Steelies." Frank had first taught me how to play the game, and actually ended up giving me a few small marbles, a few cat's eye marbles, and a few steelies to start off my collection, along with a bag to carry them in. I still have that bag, and because I do I can say jokingly, "I still have all my marbles!"

Frank lived two doors down from my apartment on Pond Street. He was a good friend also in my second to fifth grade classes at Franklin Elementary School as well as 7th and 8th grade at Grant Junior High.

I remember Frank being yelled at in front of my second grade class by Ms. Brown. It was if she was blowing fire out of her mouth due to the smell and volume. He told me her breath was so awful he felt sick. She had a foul odor. It was as if she never brushed her teeth, shaved her armpits, or used deodorant.

I recalled years later that I only ever once saw her walking on the streets of Syracuse one time. She had to have been at least ninety years old.

There are two things about Ms. Brown's second grade class that I thought were odd:

1. We did our math on small chalkboards
2. Whenever Ms. Brown wasn't looking or stepped out of the classroom, the children would color in coloring books. When I told the children I never did this in my other town where I grew up, they looked at me like I was the odd one.

Fairly soon, I was given coloring books and some

crayons. I thought the whole thing was rather strange. The children would hide their coloring books in the back of their desks, and whenever she went out of the room or looked away, they colored. The funny thing is that she had to have known. To me, it was comical.

It was here in the middle of my second grade education, in this classroom, that I met many friends who I would know for most of my formal education of twelve grades: Frank Cirbus, Jimmy O'Hara, Inez Ponzo, Sarah Kharas, Vito Barletta, Kevin Maloid, etc. Most of all, I met Tony Callipari, my all-time best friend ever.

"A friend loveth at all times, and a brother is born for adversity."

(Proverbs 17:17)

The next street we moved to was Park Street, which intersected Pond Street. We moved to 1212 Park Street, where our neighbor was Linda. Linda had a daughter named Celina. Every time I think of Celina, I think of a recording on a cassette tape that my mother made concerning her name.

I still recall the moment that my mother, Angela, made the recording because I was there. I still have that same cassette player. It was simple and crude and went like this: "Celina, Celina, Celina…. Celinnaaa: F--- you!" It was the way my mother said it that made anyone who heard it laugh!

My sister Melissa will mouth these same words and we will both laugh. Again, it wasn't the derogatory word we were laughing at, but it was the tone and delivery of how my mother had said it!

I thought that our neighbor Linda was a gorgeous, sexy woman who had a sex appeal about her that got me excited anytime she was near me. I told my sister, as we told each other everything back then. If Linda was coming over, she would tease me, saying, "Oooh, Mike?!" I would always smile and say something like, "Yeah, so what?!" and my sister would have this huge grin on her face, which in turn would make me smile too.

The last summer we lived at this apartment building, I decided to grow a watermelon out in the backyard. We had started growing it in school, and then I took it home and planted in the backyard.

Well, being in the city and still leery of folks, I kept my eye on it. The sad fact was that the day that we moved, I was going to pick it but could not. All night I was real concerned about my watermelon, and for good reason: Some idiot stole it that evening. I knew I should have picked it, but how would anyone know that?

I had hoped one day to find the thief or thieves, but I never did. Someone else ate the "fruits" of my labor.

I have a feeling that these thieves have been paid back. At least that is what I believed, because it made me feel better, and who knows? I believe in the Universal Rule of Scripture that we reap what we sow.

After Park Street, we moved to Hier Avenue. We lived first at 237 Hier for some years, and then my mother's friend Debbie sold her house to us at 231 Hier Avenue, only two doors down. Our next door neighbor between those two homes was Jean Tarbona (before she married my cousin John Logan over twenty-five years). Debbie had a daughter, Andrea, who liked my brother— and he liked her back. Debbie always thought that they would marry and then we'd be related. Andrea is divorced and living now with a woman. She has two beautiful children from her first marriage.

This was the last house we lived in before my mother sold that and moved into the same trailer park that my Uncle Richard had been living at for over thirty years. Our last tenant we had, who lived above us in the apartment, was Stanley, who had real health issues, but was good to us all.

Before we moved, my mother had remarried a second time (past tense) to my former stepfather Rocco J. Manzi Jr. They were married fourteen years, versus the thirteen years she had been married to my father Dominick. Everyone called him Rocky. He had six brothers who had been fighters named Rocky except one.

Sadly, I stayed home when my mother got married to my stepfather Rocky. They had gone to the Justice of the Peace in Syracuse. My Uncle Richard, my sister, my brother, my grandmother, and my mother's friend Sue all went. I just sulked at home on the couch. Believe me, I did feel bad that I had not gone, and was told to stay on the couch till they got back except to use the bathroom.

Thank God, my parents had an amicable relationship after their divorce. My dad also got along with Rocco, too.

Rocky's one brother, Patrick, had been a local light

welterweight champion in boxing. I may be wrong on the weight division, and I have no details of the history, but I saw the newspaper clipping once, years ago, over at his home. Pat's wife, Chris had a store, "Deco-Beads," which sat below their home at the corner of Butternut Street and Carbon Street. She sold beads, as well as things that she made with beads.

One time, in the first five years that my mother was married to Rocco, when I was about thirteen years old, something happened to him that I only had seen before in movies. He got shot by someone in a Black Muscle car (had a loud muffler) that drove slowly by the first house we lived in, at 237 Hier Avenue. The police never found the shooter.

I was behind Rocky with my Mother on the left side of him. We all heard a car outside, and he opened the door. While standing there, we heard a loud "bang!" All of a sudden, Rocky says, "Oh, no, I think I've been shot!" Of course, my Mom was hysterical, calling the police and ambulance. I was right behind him. They never got the bullet out of his hamstring area, and he always had to let the airports know this fact.

Another sad incident was my father got caught shoplifting at Fay's Drugs at the corner of Lodi and Butternut Streets in Syracuse. My stepfather went down to the store and bailed him out. No charges were filed. My father could never show his face there again.

I also had my stepfather discovered once after I came home with books I had stolen at a bookstore in Shop City (a shopping center) in Eastwood, New York. He took me back, no charges filed, and I could never show my face again. Like father like son, unfortunately.

CHAPTER 17

Tony and I have been the greatest of friends for over forty-two years. I have lived away from New York since my late twenties. I always make a point to visit my best friend, Antonio Callipari every year I go to visit Syracuse. Tony, was also called "Tony Pepperoni," or "Tony Bologni," and more like a brother to me.

Tony and I were "thick as thieves," as we were extremely close. In fact, as busy as my friend Tony Callipari may be in his life, he still makes an effort to keep in touch with me via phone or text.

And the man is busier than I probably have been in my own life for a few reasons. He has a forty-plus hour a week job for the past twenty-plus years. It's been over thirty years since I had my own real "on the books" job.

He's married to a woman named Kathy who, for some years now, has had a slipped disc. He's been married around fifteen-plus years, together twenty- four-plus years. She was working for a dentist as a dental hygienist, working too many hours, which ended up causing her injury.

Tony and Kathy have a son, Tony Jr., and he also has two

stepchildren (one of them lives with he and his Kathy). He has two dogs, a few vehicles, and a modular home in the country that he is continually working on. Trees, a garden, a garage, a woodshed, and grass to cut alone would keep any man busy. Tony's done a lot of landscaping around his home. Add to that a wife, three children, a full-time job, and you have a recipe for being busy! He is a hard worker!

I was also was at Tony's wedding. It was a nice time, and I got the chance to dance with quite a few of the ladies who were there at the reception.

While growing up whenever Tony's mom was making dinner and I was hanging out with him at night, they would set a plate for me at their table to share. I felt like I was part of the family. We both loved each other's family. Tony had a crush on my sister and vice versa: I had a crush on two of his sisters: Rosa and Natalie. Tony had three sisters and one brother. They pretty much all lived at home until they got married. That's definitely an Italian tradition, for children to stay home until marriage. Tony's mother was German/Polish, and Tony's father was pure 100% Italian, born straight from Italy.

One night, when we were about fifteen years old, Tony, me, and this guy Joe (who Tony knew) went out drinking. There was a full moon out, and it looked larger than usual. We were walking that evening and ended up going to North High School on Pond Street, when we heard a bunch of teenagers drinking in one of the old Forts on the playground of the old high school! Someone played music on their boom box.

Tony looked at Joe and me and said (while staring up at the full moon), "Hey, ya know, I have a bad feeling about tonight. Someone is going to turn on the other two."

Well, we began to drink with some guys we knew at the fort. I was only slightly buzzed (I wasn't a heavy drinker, like my friends), but Joe and Tony and a few others got really drunk. As the old saying goes, "Man takes a drink, drink takes a drink, drink takes the man!"

Tony and this guy Kenny White (we'd known him for years in our elementary and junior high schools) started a fight over something stupid called "being drunk." It was a real brawl that lasted what seemed like a good half hour or so. Blood flew everywhere. Both of them were staggering the whole time. As far as who ended up winning, I would say my friend Tony won.

The strange thing about the fight was that, by the time it was over, they both started apologizing to each other. They even hugged in the end and said they were sorry tearing up!

I witnessed another fight when Tony and I were working at Michael's Pizza. It was located on Park Street around the corner from Tony's parents, who lived at 150 John Street. Our friend Carmen Spoto was manager of this pizza shop.

You see, this guy I graduated with, Alex came to the shop one evening. He kept begging me to give him one of my psychotropic pills? At this time in my life I had been out of the US Army a year, and was on psychotropic medicine. How he found out, I will never know. I told him that if I gave him one, he might end up in the hospital, and I told him to go away. He kept asking and wouldn't leave, so I gave him one.

I said to him, "Don't bother me if you end up in the hospital, man!" Well, he ended up in the hospital one night. He came back to Michael's Pizza one evening and told me I should pay him because he got sick. What an idiot!

"Uh, no man, go screw yourself! I told you not to bother me if you got ill," I said.

Carmen was there that night and told him, "Get out of here! I'm not going to tell you again?!"

Alex (being the jerk he was) kept pleading with me. Carmen was at the counter (he was a tall and big guy with long arms) and this Alex was peering inside the counter, trying to look for me. Big mistake. Some punks just need to learn a lesson.

Carmen hit Alex so hard he knocked him into the doorway. One might say the next century! Blood flew everywhere, a tooth flew out of his mouth, and Alex landed on the floor, dazed and confused. Instead of leaving the shop like a normal person, he got up and ran toward Carmen. Carmen, this time standing in the front of the counter, hit him with such force he landed on the sidewalk outside with a bloody eye. Carmen walked out the door and told him to go home.

The whole time this was happening, Carmen was calm as a cucumber, and Tony and I just watched in awe. Here was a guy trying to extort money from me after I gave him a pill for free—with a warning—but didn't listen. Talk about an unwise person. I never saw the point in fighting unless for a good reason. This was a good reason. I thought "fighting" for my country was more intelligent than a bar fight.

"To each His own." This is one of my mother's favorite sayings, and a phrase that seems to pop in my head quite often in my inner thoughts. My father had a saying he used to say to me often as well.: "Keep it in your pants!" It was great advice, but he did not follow it himself. Why give advice to your son if you yourself do not use your own advice. Hence the saying, "Do as I say, not as I do!" They call that "hypocrisy," and as for my father, he didn't listen to his own advice. But none of us are perfect; I'm just pointing out facts.

At times my friend Tony and I would would go roller skating to try and pick up women. Our favorite hangout was at the clubs at Syracuse University, near Marshall Street. One of the clubs we enjoyed in particular was Sutter's Mill, otherwise known back then as Slutter's Mill.

One night at Sutter's Mill, when I was sixteen years old, everything was going fine, until I opened my mouth and messed it up. I had just gotten my license and went out to celebrate that night, with my friends Tony, Scott Flanagan, Dan Ryan, and Michael Farino.

I got in while my friends, who were older than me, had to be carded. Right away I went to the dance floor, because they were playing a good Michael Jackson song. My friends went to get a table off to the left of the bar and a few pitchers of beer, laughing as they saw me leave for the dance floor. Out of the four of us, I was the smooth-talking dancer.

After leaving the dance floor, I went up to the bar and bought a mixed drink. I was about to go over to the table where my friends were, but these three female college students walked by me and started to speak to me. In fact, one of them, a gorgeous brunette, said, "Hey there good-looking, whatcha got cooking?"

In true Hollywood style, I bravely took her in my arms, dipping her and kissing her full on the lips. I kissed her for a moment (it seemed like a while. Ya know, time flies when you're having fun!) and then released her.

I was a little breathless from it, and she looked in awe at me, at how I had made her feel from my kiss. Without bragging, I have never had any complaints on my kissing a woman. We kissed a moment longer, and I felt almost speechless.

"Is that hair on your chest?!" she asked.

"Yes, it is," I said smugly, as she placed her hand inside my sweater.

We started talking, and soon I was stupidly telling her I was sixteen years old. She insisted I was older than sixteen, and then I mindlessly showed her my driver's license.

"Oh, my goodness, I just kissed a minor!?!"

She looked at her two friends who were next to us, watching the whole interaction.

"Let's go girls!"

The young women laughed while walking away sexily as if to say, "Man, you missed out, sweetie!"

Slightly buzzed and upset that I had opened my big mouth, I ran to the table where my buddies were all drinking, took one of the full pitchers of beer, and dumped it right down the sink in the men's room.

My friends Tony and Scott followed me, trying to stop me, but I was too fast for them. I paid for another round of beer, and we all got to speaking about what just happened with that nineteen-year-old gorgeous brunette I had in my arms. I had ruined my opportune moment.

Of course, years later, looking back on my life as a Christian, at all that carousing around, drinking, and looking to have sex, I realized it wasn't at all ever a good thing in this life anyway. I killed a lot of brain cells as well as wasted a lot of money and time. As much as I saw it back then as a missed opportunity, that "fun" could have killed me: something as sinister as "AIDS." Like the New York lottery says, "Hey, ya never know!" All of us were young once and did things were ashamed of now.

CHAPTER 18

My friend Tony and I often headed near a shopping center called Shop City in the Eastwood area to play some pool. Tony had a real skill for playing this game. Every time we were out drinking or playing pool, the band Journey would come on the jukebox, playing one of their very well-known and highly requested songs. Songs like "Don't Stop Believing," "Open Arms," "Sherry," etc. Def Leppard was another popular band back then that we enjoyed listening to.

Several times my friends Tony, Scott, Dan (nicknamed "Dan the Man"), and I would drink on weekends. There were plenty of parties during high school. Sometimes, when my friends would come over, I would brush them off because I had to study. We had a lot of parties at our friend Mike Farino's home at 165 Clifton Place in the Eastwood, New York area.

One weekend, my friends' Tony, Scott, and Dan had asked me (the youngest of them all) to go into a liquor store and buy Seagram's Seven and Jack Daniel's for them. At the time, they weren't old enough. Being the brave fool that I was back then, I did it. The crazy thing is that the guy behind the counter never asked to see my ID. I actually looked like I was old enough!? When you're young that seems like a good thing, but as you get older it's a bad thing. I was about thirteen years young.

The next day I found out that Scott, Dan, and Tony had gotten really drunk. They were so drunk that they crawled a mile on their hands and knees to get home. I had not drunk very much and Mike Farino's father had given me a ride home.

Mr. Farino was quiet most of the time, but he expressed his concern for us drinking so much. Strange coming from him, since I think he drank daily. He never really spoke too much, but his wife, Donna (who—small world—went to school with my mother), was the one with the gift for gab.

Lots of times we would bring the beer or keg to my house, because my mother was cool about it. She would at times bring us blankets, a heater, and cups. She would tell my friends and me to go out and have fun "sowing our oats." I did all my "experimenting and riotous living" when I was still young.

I always let my mother know where I was going so she wouldn't worry. I knew that a lot of teenagers back then probably thought there was something childish in letting my mother know where I was at all times, but to me it was simply being safe.

Even as an adult, when I am traveling long distance I let others I know where I am going. If something ever happened to me on a trip somewhere, and no one knew. folks would worry if I became missing. I had what I believed was the greatest Mom ever, and even my friends agreed about this fact. I didn't need her to worry any more than she did as a mom!

Tony and I had some real crazy times together, but all in all we have remained friends to this day now well over forty-two years.

One time I met a woman named Yvonne Reaume. I don't recall how I met her, but I began to write her letters. My friends Tony, Scott, and I went to her high school graduation party and were truly welcomed. We had a very good time, and then it was time to go home.

Let's just say that by the time I had gotten home they had to carry me inside the house. I fell right into the lap of my stepbrother, Little Rock's girlfriend Beth, face first into her crotch. Talk about feeling stupid and happy at the same time! I was quickly shoved away by my stepbrother.

Embarrassing. I never got that drunk again! I had wasted too much time praying to the porcelain god, as they say, when you hover over the toilet because you drank too much alcohol! Many folks I went to school with are still doing this today. It didn't take me thirty-plus years to learn this nonsense. Just a few years!

CHAPTER 19

Tony had a job making money before I did. There was a Peter & Son's Dry Cleaners on the corner of his block at Park and John Street, where my father used to go for his dry cleaning. It was there that Tony first made $2 dollars for sweeping the back room, which he did as often as he could. Still, it was a job!

In winter, we would shovel snow for money. We delivered pizza on the north side. Of all the people I knew growing up and driving food or people for a living, my friend Tony was the best. He knew the streets of Syracuse better than any other person I knew growing up!

In the 80's I believe Tony made the best pizza in Syracuse, NY. He worked at 3 pizza shops, but I only recall two of them: "Michael's Pizza" and "Rosie's Corner." I also worked for 2 shops too. For the past 45 years "Varsity Pizza" where a Greek woman makes what I consider the best pizza!

Another activity we both enjoyed was to go to Tony's grandparents' camp in New York and sleep out in tents by the waters of Sandy Pond. One time we were in a tent with his sister Natalie and a few girls who lived next to our camping area. I made out with one of the girls. They decided for fun they would try to levitate my body. Using the tips of their fingers on the edge of my body, I lie not: They *did* levitate my body! Don't believe me? You could ask my friend Tony or his sister Natalie.

Tony and I had ridden our ten-speed bikes everywhere before we got a car. Tony again was the first to drive a car of his own. His first car was a 1973 Nova. We both loved this great piece of American machinery that any teenager could work on. It was truly a great vehicle and simple to work on.

The first car I bought upon getting out of the U.S. Army was a real nightmare for a mechanic! It was a 1980 Oldsmobile Omega. I never saw so many wires sticking out of an engine before. I paid $1,250 for this car. My father helped me to pick this piece of crap. I have been driving a foreign car for the past thirteen-plus years, and I would never go back to an American car if you paid me. Since I have been driving a Subaru, I haven't had any problems, but my relatives who buy American-made cars seem to have issues at times with their vehicles.

Another thing we did as teens was funny. Tony had a neighbor who lived four doors down, on the same side of John Street. He was growing pot in the front yard of his house.

Tony, David "Scott" Flanagan (another friend of ours), and I all spotted it one day while walking to Tony's house. We all agreed to "take" this pot (which was illegal) the next evening. Strange that an herb that cures cancer is illegal, while alcohol, which kills thousands each year, is legal.

We agreed to steal this marijuana in the wee hours of the next morning. It was around 1 a.m. when we all ran from Tony's porch to the pot plants and pulled them out of the ground. We bagged them and put on Tony's porch. The funny thing is that we were all "naked," as a sort a double dare activity we had agreed upon. We all laughed our ass off for a long time at what we had done. I believe laughter is the greatest medicine. Scott took the pot home, dried it, and then we used it whenever we wanted some. Scott's dad ended up finding it and gave it to the local police.

What kind of man does that and tells the police that it was his son's?

We have gone through many trials and tribulations together, enjoying both the good and bad times in our lives. But once your youth is gone, there's no turning back. You can't turn back time (unless you're Cher), or can you? I believe Time Travel is possible, and that the U.S. government has such "projects."

A lowpoint in Tony and I's friendship was that a friend of ours who died shortly after his graduation from Henninger High School, where Dan, Scott and myself all attended. (Tony, due to his address, attended Fowler High School.) Our friend, Michael Farino, graduated in 1983.

He was two years ahead of Tony and me. Mike was a hemophiliac, and in 1983 he ended up getting the HIV virus, upon receiving bad blood from a transfusion. His family sued, and this country began to test the blood from that point onward. I am glad that at least Mike's life wasn't completely in vain, and that his life served the purpose of ensuring that what happened to him would not happen to others. Sadly, it's a memory I don't think about often, except when I go back to visit friends and family every year in Syracuse. Strange thing is that my old friend Dan has lived on Michael's street (Clifton Place) for the past fifteen years, not very far from the very house that the Farinos used to own. Dan had married Tony's sister Olivia. The sad fact was that Michael Farino had suffered much in his short life. When the funeral was over, those of us who helped carry his coffin just sat around talking about him and how he made our lives special. Some of the guys had brought a beer to pour over his gravesite, something he wanted us to do. Mike's family had other tragedies following his death. I heard his sister took her life in Florida, for what reason I have no idea. Many of my friends in Syracuse who knew the family believed it was unresolved pain from the loss of her brother. Michael's brother was a real scumbag who, I heard, ended up in prison. I am not sure about Michael's parents. After Michael died, and the family moved away to Florida, I had no desire to stay in touch.

CHAPTER 20

Another great thing that happened to my good friend Tony and I was the Summer of 1981. Sadly, it was a year after my grandfather Antonio "Bully" Gugliano had died (he was nicknamed "Bully" because he was built like a bull and strong like an ox); but this was the year I met the beautiful Italian woman Theresa, and Rita her sister.

Tony had begun to sort of see Rita, and I began to date Theresa. I don't think it ever really got too romantic with Rita and Tony. I was thirteen years old, soon to be fourteen that year in October. Theresa was seventeen years old and going to be a senior at Henninger, while Tony and I were going to be freshmen. She lived near me in Syracuse at 203 Park Street.

Tony and I swam a lot at Schiller Park that year (only a few blocks from my house) and started a club we called the Gooching Club. Of course, we were the only ones in it. But if we were hanging out with other male friends, they would participate too. We would be swimming in the pool when it was crowded, and we would grab ("gooch") a girl's butt underwater and swim away as fast as we could without getting caught.

I know what you're thinking, but hey, we were just kids having fun. There wasn't anyone getting hurt, though it might have bothered the girl for being "touched." Frankly, if a girl had grabbed my butt underwater it would be flattering, but I am sure most girls would think differently. Compared to living in 2018 and what goes on today(like cyber bullying; Students sex with Teachers; School Shootings), that was really harmless.

One day we were about to leave the pool when I spotted Theresa and her sister Rita in the pool. Tony saw them too, and we quickly came up with a plan: Tony would push me into the pool right where Theresa was standing. I ending up being close to her, but no one was hurt, and we began to chat. Honestly, Theresa was the most beautiful woman I had ever laid eyes upon, at least up to that point in my life. She is still in the top three most beautiful women I have ever been with in my life.

CHAPTER 21

In the summer of '81, Theresa was the first woman I dated with whom I went farther than second base, as they say.

First base is kissing, second base is touching, third base is heavy petting, and, of course, what we called a "home run" is otherwise known as sex. I never scored a home run until I was in my first year in the Army (I was 17.5 years young when I lost my virginity); but with Theresa I came real close.

Theresa was my first love. They say you never forget your first love. Three years later, I was reading *Forever* by Judy Blume about first love.

Theresa used to babysit a few blocks away from her home, and I met her there. Of course, the reason I went over was to make out with her and speak with her for two hours. One time while we were kissing, I got to kissing and nibbling her ear. I found out this got Theresa really turned on.

The next moment she pulled down her pants and whispered in my ear, "Play with me!" You talk about one excited young man. This was totally new territory to me.

I played with her until she had an orgasm. Now, I know some people reading this might not think too highly of this activity for a thirteen-year-old to be partaking in, but hey, I was young and at this point in my life I was not a Christian. So, give me a break.

I am definitely not perfect in my life, and I am sure all those who may be reading my story could say the same. There's only one man who ever walked the face of the Earth who was perfect: the Creator, the Savior, Jesus Christ, the Lord!

Theresa to me was one of the most beautiful women I had ever been with in my life, and I feel richer for the experience. She is also the first woman in my life with whom I French-kissed. She actually taught me how to perform that kiss. Up to this point in my short life, there wasn't anything better than kissing Theresa in the summer-time sun!

At the corner of James and Dewitt Streets in Syracuse stood a bank. This bank had an underground drive-way for folks conducting their banking business. It had closed down some years earlier, and that is where I first French-kissed her. So, whenever I wanted to make out with her, I would put up my two fingers like a peace sign, signaling that we should go there.

I am almost fifty years old, and I would say I have waited a long time in my life for someone good to come along, whom I would yearn to kiss and fall in love with again.

After the Summer was over she went back to dating some twenty-year-old "jerk."

This guy frankly didn't deserve her, but he had a car and a job that I couldn't exactly compete with at the time. I found out years later that she dumped him not long after me, and some years later after that summer she had gotten married and had some children. I found out on Facebook (long ago I deleted my page. I have no social media) that her sister Rita died sadly of cancer. Rita had some children, but not sure if she was married?

My sister, Melissa, had seen Theresa once in Believer's Chapel Church and spoke to her. The last I heard, she was working for Wegmans supermarket in North Syracuse. For years now, I have wanted to see her again, even if it's simply to say "hello." I want to look into her eyes and relive those memories from my youth.

One of the life's greatest pleasures is being young, and yet many never realize this fact until they are older. I knew this truth, and if I was able to travel back in time, I would go back to that particular moment in time when I dated Theresa!

CHAPTER 22

I actually did quite well in my school career, being on the honor roll every single year I attended school.

After graduating from elementary school, I went to Grant Junior High. While I was in eighth grade, the school's name became Grant Middle School, and when they built a new wing they named it after Janitor Bruce Capriotti, who worked there for thirty-three years.

They had quite a ceremony with the Mayor Lee Alexander (who ended up going to a country club jail for a time because of embezzlement); Principal Nick Abdo; the art teacher (don't recall the man's name. He wore glasses and had long white hair in a ponytail); Mr. Weil, my home room teacher; Bruce Capriotti, the janitor; and me.

Picked out of the entire student body of both seventh and eighth grades, I was responsible for presenting an art painting (done by the art teacher) to Bruce Capriotti, with a plaque of commemoration on the occasion of the new wing being named after him.

I had a very interesting home room teacher named Mr. Weil. One time, he got up on a table and yelled, "Repent,

Repent, you sinners!" He also had in his classroom a huge video camera—the kind you see in studio newsrooms that operate like a movie camera.

I ended up using this huge camera in the class whenever he stepped out of the room. I used to record some of the activity in the room. I also filmed scenes making students disappear. It was kind of cool, and the students thought so, too. Why it was in the room was a mystery to me. I wonder what ever happened to that footage?

In seventh grade I joined the cross-country and track teams, coached by Mr. Gardner, who was a seventh grade science teacher. I really didn't care for his class, but I enjoyed the running. We used to run to his house, pick up his dog "Red," and then run back to Grant.

I met a guy named Richard Murasky in my grade who ran on both the cross-country and track teams. Richard and I joined an after-school club that had the goal of running an extra 300 miles above and beyond what we ran with the cross-country team. Richard and I both received a T-shirt with "The 300 Mile Club" on it. We were the only two students to participate.

The first time I participated in any sport is when I joined a tiny tot football league called the Lemoyne Dolphins. Years later I would mention this to someone, stop talking, and they would ask the question, "You played football for the Dolphins in the seventies?" "Yeah," I would say. Later I would let them in on the joke, telling them it was the "Lemoyne Dolphins."

I believe I joined the football team when I was around

twelve years old. I played both center (my main position) and middle linebacker. The guy who played quarterback, named Commisso, was the son of Virginia Commisso, a friend of my mother's years later.

The first time I ever had the wind knocked out me took place during a play gone wrong during practice. It failed to fool the whole team but myself, and I caught the guy with the ball. His foot was caught in my chest.

Talk about pain! My father had actually driven me that day to this particular practice. He congratulated me for having read the defense better than anyone. I only played for one season, but it wasn't for me! That one season that I ended up playing we made it to the Championship Game, but the other team cheated and we lost due to their unsportsman-like conduct.

I won my share of ribbons while running with the cross-country and track teams, as well as three trophies and commendation certificates that I received during the first three years of high school. I also won four or more Certificates of Honor for high school Italian fairs from grades ninth to eleventh grade.

When I was twelve years old, I joined the Boy Scouts. The meetings were held very close to my home at 237 Hier Avenue. I had gone through two levels of Boy Scouts, and I also designed the handkerchief that our Troop 23 wore!

Our troop held a contest to see whose design for Troop 23's handkerchiefs would be picked. If you won, your design would be used and you would receive a free handkerchief. They took my design and sold the troop my idea, receiving all the money. It kind of sucks, because over the years that design of mine was copied in many other logos.

When I was in the Boy Scouts, another incident occurred as I was trying to get my merit badge for first aid. The instructor, Ken, was apparently a fricking pedophile, and all those boys he was around were in danger.

You see, when I went up to him in a room all alone, he pulled down his pants and underwear. I looked away and said, "Uh, what the hell are you doing?!"

"I was just going to show you the pressure points on the body!" he said, looking at me with a damn hard-on!

I ran the heck out of the room and said, "Never mind! I will do it another time!"

He yelled, "Okay, Michael ... come on back! I will pull up my pants!"

I slowly walked back and he tried to touch my body to show me the pressure points again, and I said, "Get your damn hands off me! You're sick!"

I took off running and ran the heck out of the building. One of the Scout Masters tried to stop me to ask what was wrong, but I kept running, never looking back. I went back another time and told the Head Scout Master. They ended up firing this scumbag. I did get a first aid badge anyway, because I told them if I didn't receive it that I would tell the police.

They agreed, and a different leader gave me the badge. I told my mom and stepfather about it, and they said I had done the right thing. Years later I called his wife and told her about it. Of course, she didn't care and she didn't believe me.

Before that event had happened, I recall a few good times in the Boy Scouts.

One time we participated in a winter contest with a sled and gear, following a course through the woods. The first troop that made it to the finish line would win a trophy. We didn't win, but we did end up getting badges that had the name of that particular Winter Jamboree and the year it happened, which was 1979. We also had quite the adventure in the woods with that sled. We were given a map with clues to find the way to the finish line. I also enjoyed participating in a bowling contest. I got a badge for that as well. It said Hiawatha Council BSA (Boy Scouts of America) Bowl-a-Thon. We also made wax molds out of our hands, which was cool even though they didn't last long at all.

When I was around thirteen years old, I used to frequent a bookstore not too far from my maternal grandparents' house, in the Shop City Mall in the Eastwood area. For about two months I would go to this bookstore, and on six different occasions stole about ten books each time I went there. I had been a book- worm since I was in fourth grade, and have been one ever since.

One day I came home with about twelve books, and my stepfather asked me where I got them. He knew I was lying when I told him I bought them.

He drove me back to the bookstore in Shop City and

made me apologize to the store. I told them I was very sorry and I would never come in the store again. I never did go back, and the bookstore never pressed any charges because I gave them back the books.

CHAPTER 23

When I graduated from Anthony A. Henninger Senior High School, I had a 90 average for all four years, and I only had missed four days of school the entire time. I also graduated Henninger in the top fifty students with not just one diploma, but with a second diploma called the New York State Regents Diploma. I earned it for taking college-level courses throughout high school. I also received a silver laminated card for my great attendance record. It stated 97% —I missed only four days out of 724 days of high school.

In fact, I was the only person other than my Uncle Richard in my immediate family to graduate high school the old-fashioned way: something I am still very proud of. My brother, sister and nephew all received their high school equivalent diplomas. My parents never graduated. My mother made it only through eighth grade, and my father was in eleventh grade when he left school. Sadly, I don't believe either of them ever read an entire whole book in their lives.

I enjoyed high school. My mother always used to tell us children, "School is the best time of your life!" As I grew older, I have totally agreed with her on this thought! Despite my best friend Tony Callipari having to attend Fowler High School, we still hung out on the weekends whenever we could.

I have one bad memory from my days at Henninger High School. When I was in the twelfth grade, a guy in my class named Sam Gotsis, for no reason whatsoever, spit in my face during the lunch hour. I used a handkerchief to wipe off my glasses. This was a disgusting thing to do to me, and I asked him, "What the hell did ya do that for?" He was silent. I never found out even to this day why he did this. I asked him once on Facebook (I deleted my page in 2017) about the incident. He apologized and said he didn't remember doing that. How do you forget spitting on someone as a senior in high school. Well, I had forgiven him, but not forgotten what he had alone done to me. I think he thought I would hit him. I believe he was looking for a fight. Juvenile acts for immature juveniles. Most of my life I have had to be more mature than those around me.

Maybe he got the idea to do this from Scott Travers (nicknamed "The Devil" in the '85 yearbook), the bully that he was? I never understood it, and I simply told him he was a jerk as I walked away. The students around us looked at both of us, wondering if there was going to be a fight. I recall a few girls got really disgusted at what Sam did and gave him the evil eye as they walked by him.

Sam may have changed as he got older, but frankly he was considered by many to be very immature! I dealt with enough bullies growing up, since they seemed to be everywhere.

I also recall a time when Tony and I were twenty years old, when we had decided to go to Oswego, New York. Within an hour we had met two really cute girls, I think at a laundromat! We talked them into going to a room with us, as we had some beer and pot.

I think I got the cuter one, but the woman who Tony was with wasn't bad either. By the time it was over, we had a beer or two each, smoked some pot, and had sex with them. In the beginning, the woman and I were trying to have sex in the shower, while Tony was having sex in the bed on the left side of the room.

It was logistically difficult for me and the woman I was with to have sex in the shower, and so went to use the other bed (there were two beds in the room). We called out to Tony and the other girl (I don't recall the women's names) that we were going to use the other bed.

Talk about a funny picture, with one couple humping away on one bed, and the other couple humping away on the bed next to it. We at first were cracking up but continued having sex anyway. We all had a great time and added another juvenile memory to our minds. I recall years later telling Tony, because he forgot. Of course, there have been things he remembered that I forgot, too!

As far as the drugs that Tony and I ever did were: alcohol, cocaine (only three months), magic mushrooms (maybe twice), hash (once), marijuana, and we tried acid once only. Sadly, with the money we spent on all those things we could have bought a car or house with cash! It's not something we are proud of, but we came through it all alive. Some folks I knew back then still are doing those same juvenile things.

When I was a freshman in high school, I started dating this woman named Patti Warner. Now, at the time I had really fallen in love with her, but she had these walls up around her heart and mind that, despite me being the decent, caring, loving gentleman that I am. Those walls weren't torn down until after we broke up in tenth grade sometime.

She had told me after graduation, after I returned home from the U.S. Regular Active Army, that she had loved me back then. I asked her why she never told me, but she doesn't understand why. She believes, perhaps, I would not have loved her back. She was wrong, because that's what I had been doing all along. There was a lot of dysfunction for her at home, sadly.

She was heading into the military while I was getting out. She already spoke in military terms with phrases like, "That's a wrong answer, soldier!" Looking back, maybe that was a good thing. I will never know.

What I do know is that Patti married, he was abusive, and she got divorced. I would have never been abusive to her. Though it's probably a good thing that we didn't get together, because we were too young. Looking back on these kinds of memories, I always think, "What if?" I do sometimes think back on such events in my life and wonder what would have happened in my life.

What would have happened if all worked out in my

first marriage? Would I still be married to Maria today and living in Maine?

Maria married a third time after me. But one thing I know: She was my first true love and I was her first true love. She told me that I had the most handsome jaw. I was as loyal to her as any woman I was ever with, and I would have died for Maria. Like stepping in front of a train for her love.

Maine was a lovely place to live, though it has very cold winters. We experienced the 1998 Ice Storm of New England. For fourteen days, we could not drive anywhere. The very day it started to snow, I began putting together a cigar-shaped wood stove that someone from the church we were attending, Emmanuel Community Church (and where stepdaughter Jaimie Lee was going to school), had given me. Well, after about six hours I had put it together!

The reason it took so long is because it was in such bad shape, and I had to rig it to some degree, which was trickier than I thought it would be. I thought when I began putting it together it would only take a few hours.

We used it to heat the house (we had a forced hot air furnace, but it ran on electricity, which we did not have for those two weeks), as well as to cook our meals. It sounds cozy and romantic, but it wasn't exactly!

Two weeks after the ice storm started, we drove through a winter wonderland with tons of snow, and trees down everywhere. The main roads were decent, but it still took awhile to drive anywhere. There weren't too many major highways up there, really. I recall only one of them:

Interstate 95. The rest were some main routes.

CHAPTER 24

A year and a half after Patti and I had broken up, at the beginning of my senior year, I met an incredibly beautiful woman named Cristy. Not many folks actually even knew her, even when I brought her to the senior prom. She had issues at home. She always kept a low profile, and avoided being known. She kept her life, as they say, "under the radar."

Her father was Indian, and her mother was Italian. Talk about a great combination of ethnic groups: It made for beautiful daughters! Cristy had two sisters, Tina and Sherry. I think Sherry was the oldest one's name. Cristy was no doubt the most outwardly beautiful woman I have ever been with, and ever known.

I had met Cristy in a Burger King on Butternut Street, near Lodi Street in Syracuse. I remember when I first saw her that my heart beat faster. When I finally had the nerve to go up to her, my hands were clammy, and I was sweating some. Apparently, she had already spotted me at Henninger, but had never approached me. She said that she thought I was real handsome and wondered if I was ever going to speak to her! Imagine that!

Well, speak to her I did. I used to walk her home from her job there at Burger King and ate there just to see her. She had the most unbelievably adorable smile that stirred me up like nobody's business!

She and Theresa were the two greatest kissers I ever had the opportunity to lock lips with in my life. I would give honorable mention to Nancy in Altoona, Pennsylvania. Anywhere and whenever I could steal a kiss and hug, I would. Of all the women (not including my first ex-wife) I have been involved with romantically, she stirred up my insides more than all of them combined.

I will say that when I held her and kissed her, I got an electric shock that would start in my toes and go to my head. The only other woman with whom that happened was with my first ex-wife, Maria Dee. Her name now is Maria D. M.

With Maria, I was truly head over heels, floating on a cloud, deeply, truly, and madly in love, a love that went beyond physical, mental, and emotional understanding. With Maria, it was a far-reaching, intense, and powerfully spiritual love like no other woman before, after, or since … at least yet anyway!

I asked Cristy to the senior prom of Henninger. She said yes, and we began planning it all year. It almost didn't happen.

CHAPTER 25

I am not sure when this all happened, but I remember some time while dating her that she told me on the phone that she wanted to break up. I went over to her house to find out why.

When I got to her place, her mother, Mary, answered the door. She invited me in and saw that I was upset. Her face began to contort from reading mine.

The first words out of her mouth were, "What's wrong, Michael? Can I get you something to drink?" "Here," she pointed to a chair, "why don't you sit down?"

I explained that I had gotten a call from Cristy wanting to break up. As I began to tell her, tears starting to well up in my eyes and the flood gates began pouring out. She gave me some Kleenex and said, "Here, Michael. I'm so sorry she has put you through this. You've been so good to her."

"Yeah, I don't understand why all of a sudden she's wanting to break up?" I began to talk to her about my relationship with her daughter, and ten minutes into speaking to her, the middle daughter Tina walked in, looking strangely at me.

I told Tina also what happened, and they told me to wait. She would be home soon.

I had gone through probably about twenty tissues, blowing and wiping my nose, apologizing to them both. They told me not to worry. They were most definitely on my side and knew that good men were hard to find. Cristy's mom was divorced, and her sister Tina had broken up with several guys herself.

They basically told me that they believe I am a true find, and Cristy was probably dealing with her period. They both hugged me and told me not to cry. Both of them believed it would work out.

Finally, the sound of the door was loud enough for all of us to turn around and see Cristy coming through. She looked at me and asked, "What's he doing here?"

Her mother replied, "Cristy, what's wrong? Why are you in such a hurry, storming in here like that? You need to speak to Michael. You really hurt his feelings!"

Cristy told me to come up to her room with her. I headed upstairs with her, and both her mom and Tina were looking at me, knowing it all would be fine. They knew her better than I did, and I trusted them deep down inside.

Honestly, I don't recall all the words that were said, but after some small talk she apologized to me, wiping the tears from my eyes. She kissed me deeply and squeezed me tight. We were lying on her bed when she placed my head on her lap and she stroked my hair and head, telling me, "Shhhh, don't cry honey. Everything's going to be alright. I'm sorry. We're going to be the best-looking couple at the senior prom!"

I began to fall asleep in her lap while she was lying down on the pillow. Before too long, maybe thirty minutes later, she slowly shook me, saying, "Michael, honey, wake up babe." I slowly got up, opening my eyes and trying to refocus as she woke me.

We talked for a little while longer, then I held her as we kissed for a moment. We looked at each other, deeply into each other's eyes. She assured me all was fine and apologized again. I wished her a good night and headed down the stairway.

Her mother, Mary, and her sister Tina were downstairs watching a movie. Seeing that everything was alright, they smiled. They muted the sound and talked briefly to me.

I told them they were right, and all is fine. The amazing thing is that Mary trusted me so much she allowed me to go upstairs to her daughter's bedroom. She never let any other boys go upstairs in her daughter's bedroom alone. I was the only one. That happened a few times before with a few girls, and one woman named Josie Maheu, whose parents were French Canadian. Josie lived around the corner from me on Highland Street, on Syracuse's north side. She was supposed to graduate with my class of '85 but graduated a year earlier instead.

I gave Tina and Mary a hug and then left. They both smiled and told me, "Don't worry, be happy hon!" I took their advice to heart and walked briskly back home, thinking good thoughts! I anticipated the day that I would wow Cristy at the Henninger senior ball.

CHAPTER 26

Cristy and I were in our estimation by far the best-looking couple at the 1985 Senior Ball (or Prom) for Anthony A. Henninger High School. It ended up being at the Marriott where my mother was actually working as a waitress, but she wasn't there that night. She had worked at the Marriott, then Holiday Inn, and lastly Ramada Inn.

Despite us being the best looking, two others won King and Queen of that prom. Both of them were real stuck-up teens. The Prom Queen was Karen Z. Compared to my date Cristy Brown, she was a dog, I believed! And I thought she was a stuck-up, rich snob (others did too). The so-called King was Mike L. I always thought this guy was an idiot! I looked totally better than this guy at that time, too!

Cristy and I were not only the best looking, and most mature, but we also danced our asses off more than anyone. I remember having to wipe off the sweat, as well as the sweat off my date Cristy's body, too! She was so damn beautiful that evening!

I had really gone all the way for this prom. I bought her a dress, a corsage, rented a small stretch limo, some "Corvo" red wine from Italy, some music (on cassette tapes), and some real old-fashioned Italian charm.

I was the only guy at that prom to have bought my date a dress and got a limo. There might have been maybe one other limo, but I am pretty sure that we were the only two students there with such a ride! The limo driver was also an Italian gentleman and did a great job!

It was a really nice affair, but sadly I still had an hour left on my limo, which I ended up using with three friends of mine: Tony "Pepperoni" Callipari, David "Scott" F., and Dan "the Man" R. It was Cristy's idea that I should enjoy the last hour with my friends.

Honestly, Cristy had never been treated as well as I treated her that evening, and with all the dysfunction at her home it really confused her. So many women in this country are not used to being treated well. When a man comes along who does treat her well, it's foreign to her.

Cristy, I believe, was overwhelmed by my gentleman ways, and by the end of the evening she cried happy tears. I wiped her tears with my handkerchief. My father, grandfather and uncles all used them. I never had to buy them, as I got their second-hand hankies from my relatives.

Photos were taken there at the prom, and her mother and mine also took some photos. For years later I looked for the photo of Cristy and I that was taken at the Prom, but could not find them? The camera that I used back then was so out of date (1985), so I took it to Industrial Color Labs of Dewitt, New York, to develop a few of the pictures in 2017.

At the beginning of the evening, I pinned the corsage

onto her and placed her into the limo. I had music for the ride to set the mood, and some wonderful red Italian wine. We never finished it, and I ended up giving it to the limo driver of the limo, in addition to his cash tip. It was a small stretch white limo: real "sharp," as my mother stated.

I had a few songs played at the senior prom for us both, including "Careless Whisper" by George Michael and "No Ordinary Love" and "Smooth Operator" by Sade.

Whenever I hear these songs now, the memory of Cristy comes back. It's a sad memory, because it could have been a wonderful love if she wasn't so immature in the end. I was extremely good and loyal to Cristy, just like every other woman I was in my life. **Loyalty is a rare item in society nowadays, but there are still some of us gentlemen who think and act in a chivalrous way!**

CHAPTER 27

In the fall of 1999, while I was making a call on a payphone at the Hess Gas Station in downtown Syracuse, a black guy in a baseball cap, turned backward on his head, strolled past me on his ten- speed bike. The only thing I said out of my mouth was, "Nice bike ya got there."

He snapped back, "What'd you say? You want to steal my bike?!"

I quickly replied in a louder voice, wondering if this guy was off his rocker or hard of hearing. "No, man, I said you have a nice bike!"

"You want to steal my bike!" he yells a second time, walking closer to me. I think to myself, Why is this punk wanting to start trouble?

I thought the only way I was going to get rid of this punk was to preach to him. Right away I used the name of Christ Jesus to get rid of him. I was at the time going through my first divorce in Maine, and I didn't need any more problems.

"Do you believe that Jesus Christ died for your sins, was buried, and rose the third day?" I said.

"Uh, I can't hear you, man?!" yelling to him as he quickly turned around and started calling someone on his phone. I was relieved that this jerk was heading away from me, along with his "nice bike."

All of a sudden, as I was resting on the door of my 2004 Ford Escort, I see a ton of Syracuse police cars pull up to me in quick fashion. The actual Syracuse Police Station was a block away. They all got out of their cars and pointed their six guns in my face, with one of them yelling, "All right, put your hands up, now!!!"

I put them up and got real concerned, wondering what the hell did that scumbag tell them? "Officer, you have the wrong person!" One of them, the leader of the pack, quickly retorted to me, "Hey, shut up! And stand still there!"

"What exactly did you say to the man with the ten-speed bike?" he asked me.

"All I said was… (repeating to them the gospel of Jesus Christ found in 1 Corinthians 15: 3, and 4) and that's it. I never said I wanted to steal his bike. The guy's crazy, and a troublemaker!"

All of a sudden, the leader of the Syracuse Police in that group said to me, "Don't you say that name one more time or you'll be going to jail! Understand what I AM SAYING!" He was spitting, forcing the words out of his mouth.

The first thing that came to my mind was, "Has the world gone insane!"

He told me to hit the road and stay out of trouble.

Wow, I could not believe what just happened to me.

"Uh, no problem, Officer, I'm outta here! No problem at all!"

I thought I was in the Twilight Zone! The man who wrote that, Rod Serling, happened to live about an hour away from where I was standing. I got into my Ford and slowly pulled away.

I shouldn't talk to strangers? I heard that phrase from everyone growing up. Well, this incident finally proved why it's best not to speak to strangers.

Unbelievable that someone would do such a thing. I was truly upset after driving away. You get to the point of not wanting to reach out to others.

Another such incident, one that was even much worse, unfolded in Syracuse back in the late eighties. I once had an account at a local Federal Credit Union. I had this account since I was a veteran.

Anyway, I was on the phone at a payphone booth near the Thompson Road and James Street intersection in an area of Syracuse called Eastwood, talking to customer service about my checking account.

The woman on the phone truly messed up my account in a huge way (after the incident, I heard she was fired), and I was seriously agitated. At the time, I was on some psychotropic medicine (I call "drugs"), and I think the stress, the drugs, and the frustration from this incident caused me to get really mad, and I no doubt raised my voice to her.

I told the woman that I was going to go to the credit union and close my account out, since she could not explain a discrepancy regarding the worth of my account.

Somehow, something got "lost in translation," between what I had said and what this upset person had heard. When someone is angry, you lose your rationality. She heard something very different. I believe that she thought she heard I was "going to shoot someone"? Why she thought this will remain a mystery to me. I think when you're angry you hear only what you WANT to Hear.

Well, it was just like a movie, as I pulled into the parking lot of this financial institution right near the door. As I got out and starting walking toward the door, I saw some ladies running to the front door to lock it. According to their business hours, they should have been open for two more hours.

As I got to the front door, the two ladies locked the door saying, "Go away!"

As I pulled on the door, I yelled, "Let me in, I want to close my account!"

"Get away from the door," a woman inside yells. Everyone—the women, the customers—is looking at me like I'm some criminal.

It literally felt and looked like things were going in slow motion, and then everything abruptly came back to normal speed. I was really worried now, and thought to myself "Man, am I in trouble now or what?!" Honestly, I didn't know what the hell was about to happen, but I had an idea it had to do with law enforcement. I got into my Ford and started to drive out of the parking lot, carefully and slowly.

Just as I was barely out of the driveway, eleven police

officers, with their cars and guns pointing in my direction, blocked me. I have never seen so many Syracuse Police cars at once. This is two times now that I have had cops pointing their guns at me. And again, I was innocent! Both people thought I said something I didn't.

Proper communication in this country is important, but we have been losing that battle. Remember the famous line in the movie with Paul Newman called *Cool Hand Luke*? It was near the first half of the movie where the warden says, "What we've got here is a failure to communicate!"

In that parking lot, I stopped right away and stared in disbelief.

"Put your hands on the wheel, and don't move!" one of the police officers yelled.

Just as they put me in handcuffs and were placing me in the back of a police car, my mother and stepfather Rocco J. Manzi, Jr., arrived to help me. Can you imagine twenty-two guns pointing in your direction, aimed from eleven police cars surrounding you, because your credit union THOUGHT you said something that you actually you didn't? My first ex- wife used to say, "See, what THOUGHT got ya?!"

My mother explained that I was a disabled veteran on psychiatric meds, and I wasn't violent toward anyone. I had gotten out of the Army a Disabled Veteran 1 year 1 day after I went in the military! Disabled and labeled "Bipolar Disorder." This means having large mood swings of depression and mania. My mother kept asking for them to take the cuffs off me, which they finally did. The whole incident was unnecessary! I had to go into the credit union with the police to close out my accounts. Of course, I was asked NEVER to come back, which was fine with me.

My mother told me to make sure I took my meds.

I told her, "Sure, Mom, I always do!" I gave her a kiss and thanked Rocky and she for coming down.

Rocky was sadly all too well acquainted with such scenes, because of similar situations with his own sons and relatives. Many of the Manzi's were in trouble at one time or another, it seemed. That's something I heard when my mother first met my stepfather.

Initially you are innocent before being guilty, unless someone proves otherwise in a court of law.

Now, in America today, it seemed that you were guilty before being innocent! Like the statue of Justice with the blindfold on, which was simply showing: JUSTICE IS BLIND!!!

Now, that's true! Why? Because those in the system are blinded as humans: Blinded in sin! You have heard the phrase, "I was lost, but NOW I see?!"

An unbeliever is lost in sin, but when they trust Jesus Christ as Savior, their eyes are then opened to what is truth.

CHAPTER 28

Sometime around the age of twenty-three or twenty-four years old, I joined Bally Matrix. Most people know it as Bally Fitness Center. Before it was Bally's this building was a Jack Lalanne Fitness Center. Speaking of Jack, once when I was walking on Mansion Field Park Track in Altoona, I met a woman named Shirley Hite who used to work for him.

She said that one time she saw him drink whiskey, which sounds strange for a man who cared about what he put in his body. She had opened the first women's gym in Altoona. She said back when she opened it, very few women were interested in weightlifting for fear of building muscle.

At the time I joined, I wanted to lose 30 pounds. I weighed 185 when I started, and in two months I weighed 155. I even had female trainers wanting me to be in their aerobic classes. I was asked if I wanted a job as a trainer, and yet I had no real knowledge except how to personally train.

My body fat percentage was 3.4 at the time and was told that I needed to get some fat back on. Most bodybuilders may get to 4.5% body fat when in competition, but, according to internet research, it was rare that athletes would get to the percentage of where I was at that time.

At the time I was going to the gym twice a day. Once after breakfast and once after lunch. I simply did a circuit training of machines that hit all the major muscle groups, along with thirty to forty-five minutes' cardio before I started lifting weights. That was it, and that is how I lost the weight.

In 2013, I looked up Cristy Brown. Her mother didn't live very far from her in Linklaen, New York. This is where I had attended a small country church and taught the Bible, just a country block up on the same road where her mother was living with her second husband.

I drove from Altoona to see her and after the evening with her I drove up to Syracuse, New York, where I visited my relatives before heading back home to Pennsylvania. I didn't spend very much time with Cristy on that trip.

Cristy's father, an alcoholic and Native American (interesting how so many Indians in this country have a drinking problem), was living in the city of Binghamton, New York. I figured he wasn't doing well and I may not see him again. I found him in a bar and visited with him for about an hour. The first half hour I spoke to him in the bar, and the last half hour I spoke to him in his apartment. This was the last time I would ever speak to him again. I saw him the day after I saw Cristy in 2013 before driving back to Pennsylvania.

I had the chance to present to him the Gospel of Jesus

Christ, just as I did to Cristy when I saw her in 2013. I only hoped that they both truly trusted the Gospel I gave to them.

I had gotten a room at a local motel. After seeing Cristy's place, we decided to sleep the night at a local motel. We got caught up with each other's lives, had some dinner, and went back to the room. I had been looking forward to time in bed with her ever since I was sixteen years old.

When I was sixteen, Cristy and I were over at my bedroom in my parents' home. Things got heated while we were making out. She reached down in my pants as we passionately kissed.

There we were enjoying this marvelously terrific teenage moment, and about to have sex, when we both heard the collapsible folding door being pulled opened with the words, "Michael, where are you?!" My mother had barely gotten out the words when both Cristy and myself jumped next to each other.

Still holding her, I yelled at my mother, "Mom, please! Do you mind?!"

"Yeah, I mind. I was yelling, wondering where you were? I was worried," she said as she pulled the door shut again. "Are you going to introduce me to your girlfriend?!"

"Yeah, Mom, give us a second. You scared us!" We both got off the bed and I introduced Cristy to my mother.

"Nice to meet you, honey!" exclaimed my mother, shaking her hand.

"Nice to meet you finally, too, Mrs. Melice," Cristy said.

I corrected her, saying it was Mrs. Manzi.

"Would you like something to drink?" my mother said, offering her food and drink, because this is what most Italians do if properly raised.

"Oh, no, Mrs. Manzi. I have to be going." "Call me Angie, hon!"

Cristy smiled, thanking her anyway, and I kiss her good-bye. I tell Cristy I was really sorry, and she said to not worry. She told me she would call later.

I asked my mother WHY she walked in on us instead of yelling through the closed door. I wouldn't have walked into her room without knocking.

"Oh, don't worry," she yells. She told me to simply relax and get over it. She would have really yelled at me if I told her that. But having grown up to respect my mother, I just relax and move on.

I gave her a kiss and asked what's for dinner. "Meatloaf, Michael, alright?!"

"Yeah, Mom, I love you too!"

Thinking back on it all, my mom may have saved Cristy and me from making a big mistake in having sex, and she maybe getting pregnant. Life would not be good if that would have happened! Thanks, Mom!

CHAPTER 29

I had joined the cross-country and track teams in high school, since I had done these sports the previous two years in junior high school. I thought being a part of a team was good preparation for the military. As a freshman, I recall having Coach Nolan for the cross- country, indoor track, and outdoor track teams. Many of the guys on the team did not like him all that well.

All four years of high school, our cross-country and track Teams did quite well. No matter which season of running we were in, we put a lot of miles in preparation for the 3.2-mile cross-country races. For track and indoor track, we used to average ten-mile runs for after-school practice Monday through Friday.

Cross country usually is in the Fall Season. Many times, the running trails end up being muddy. It's due to the hundreds of boys and girls who continually stomp over the same area. Usually, by the time you are done running in a cross-country race, you're covered with dirt and mud. You start with hordes of guys and/or girls (the races are separated: girls run against girls, guys against guys), and within moments the number of runners thins out so that it's almost a single file of runners.

Points are given to each place. I can't exactly recall my stats, or those of my teammates, but usually we placed in the top sixty runners out of 150 runners. Some of our school's runners placed in the top three spots, and a small handful went onto State and National meets.

We had a good women's team for cross country and also track. The top two female runners were Christine M. and Hope W. Christine had a sister and brother who also were on the track and cross-country teams. They also did well academically! Years later, I found that Christine became a surgical doctor in sports medicine, and she sadly hadn't married. I always thought she would have made a wonderful wife and mother.

When I was on the track team at Henninger, between 1981 and 1984, we had tons of wins, and made it into the newspaper and TV spots, too. Some of the young men who were on these teams with me back then went on to score college records and several wins!

Henninger's greatest year in the field of high school track while I attended was 1983. By the way, Coach Nolan left during my first year of cross-country and indoor and outdoor track. The coach who replaced Mr. Nolan was a man who had worked previously for Christian Brother's Academy.

Mr. Riordan was quite the character and had a story that followed him wherever he went. He must have at one time had a temper. The rumor goes that he threw a young student out of a window three stories high.

What really happened, as he told it to us, was the following:

Many of these students at Christian Brother's Academy were stuck up and cocky young punks. What they needed was some good old-fashioned discipline! Mr. Riordan would be the one to show them!

What had happened was that he simply took one of the students who were acting up (he had been there ten years before this happened) and swept him up with his hands around his collar and put his body up upon the wall with his feet dangling and stated, "Merry Christmas, Mother-F----r!" The young punk student tried to sue and failed. Mr. Riordan was asked to resign. The young student left and never came back.

What ended up happening by 1983, just two years after he had become our new cross-country and track coach, was that many great runners heard how well he was coaching and began joining! Soon, we had some of the greatest athletes that our high school had ever seen. Mr. Riordan was always recruiting. He had a way of making students feel at ease and comfortable.

In 1983, our track team became State Champions, and both the indoor track team as well as the cross- country team had a great year. Some of those very athletes went on to play for professional sports teams. One of them who was on our track team was Ray Seals, who became a pro football player. Ray had a brother, Mark, with whom I graduated from Henninger in 1985. Ray Seals played as a walk-on for the Pittsburgh Steelers in the late nineties; he even played for Pittsburgh in the 1996 Super Bowl.

Syracuse, New York, produced many outstanding sports stars as well: Jim Brown, Floyd Little, Art Monk, Dick Butkis, Tim Green, Ernie Davis (all these guys played for Syracuse University football); Tom Tuori (he was supposed to run the trials for the 1988 Olympics but got in an accident and went on to become an attorney, I believe); and Kevin Anderson from our track team, who earned high school and college high jump records! To this day Kevin's records are intact. The number of great sports stars from Syracuse is too numerous to mention.

The events in track in which I competed were: 800 meters, 1 mile, 2 mile, 1-mile race walk, and sometimes a relay race like the 4 X 400 meters or 4 X 800 meters. When I ran cross country, my best time was around 13:35 to 14 minutes for 3.1 miles. My best ever 100- meter dash was 11.7 seconds. My best ever 400-meter dash was 54 seconds. My best ever mile was 4:55. My best 2 mile was around 11 minutes.

The best 1-mile race walk I ever finished was 7:33.3 minutes, in the 1982 Onondaga County City Track Meet, where I came in second place behind my team mate Michael Mitchell. He went on to make the U.S. Navy a career, where he met his wife and had a child or two.

The guy I beat, who finished in third place, was from Christian Brother's Academy—which was really great, since Coach Riordan got a chance to look good in front of the school he was asked to leave. It was one of the greatest all-time memories for me in my high school track days!

When I told my mother how I had passed this guy in the last 100 meters of the race, she responded that she never had been to any of my races. I felt bad about this years later?! I never invited my mother to any of these meets because I thought it would be embarrassing for me and I wouldn't be able to concentrate if she was there?!

Mr. Riordan our new coach himself was quite the amazing runner. When he came to the school to coach, he was already in his fifties. He participated in some really prestigious marathons, like Boston, Philadelphia, and New York City.

CHAPTER 30

While I was in the eleventh grade, I decided to join the U.S. Army. There were three main reasons why I joined:

1. I could get money for college.

2. I would get into great shape.

3. My grandfather was a World War II hero. His troop was at Iwo Jima, where the iconic raising of the American flag took place.

Frankly, I think it was crazy that my brother didn't do at least two years, just to get college tuition. Honestly, I think my uncle and brother just were not cut out for such a vocation. I don't think my brother really liked authority, and my uncle just wasn't this kind of a guy.

I ended up joining the military early in eleventh grade in the delayed entry program to help me receive more time on my actual regular active file while serving.

I was looking forward to this next chapter in my life, and at the same time I was really nervous about the whole experience.

CHAPTER 31

I chose to enjoy the first half of the 1985 summer with friends, and the second half preparing for my departure into the U.S. Regular Active Army. I was very apprehensive about this next adventure in my life.

The two things I focused on as physical preparation for the Army were calisthenics and running.

I believe the single one exercise you can do to transform your entire body is the Push-up. Probably the three greatest exercises for overall health would be the Push- up, the Pull-up, and the Squat. These three exercises cover the entire physique. The only problem is, How many of us truly want to do them every week?

The time soon approached before it was my: first time away from home, first real important job, first time away from family and friends in my entire short life. I was merely seventeen years old upon entering the Army. In two months, I would be eighteen years old.

The one friend whom I would miss the most was my best friend, Antonio "Pepperoni" Callipari. Without a doubt, Tony was the greatest friend I have ever had in my life, and though we don't see or speak to each other as often as we once did, we still keep in touch. He will always be the greatest friend this life will ever have offered to me. He also is a believer in Jesus Christ.

CHAPTER 32

It would be an adventure, but I was somewhat apprehensive, since this was my first time away from home. I tried to have as much fun as I possibly could with friends, especially my best friend, Tony Callipari.

As the end of the summer approached, I was getting anxious about the day I would venture out into the world on my own into the United States military.

Before getting on the bus, I spent the night at the Sheraton Hotel in Liverpool, New York. I wasn't really into doing any last minute "partying on the town," as many other guys were doing.

Frankly, I was nervous as hell and simply tried to get some sleep as early as possible, even though there was quite a lot of noise going on that evening. Most of the guys staying there were heading into the military the next day. I was ready to get serious with the next phase in my life.

Upon getting ready in the morning, I looked into the mirror, thinking how these were my last moments as a civilian, before getting sworn into the U.S. Army. We boarded a bus for a long, uncomfortable ride. The driver got lost along the way. I was upset, because the last thing I wanted to happen was being late for my first day in the U.S. Army.

We finally got to the destination, and Basic Training wasn't the first place I ended up. We stopped at the Reception Center, where all of us got off with our bags. We stood with the bags by our side at attention, with our belongings next to us, as we waited further orders.

Finally, some Sergeant came along with a Spec 4 NCO (Non-Commissioned Officer) running alongside him. We were led single file in a march to our quarters. I don't recall too much about the Reception Station except a lot of drill work: marching, saluting, push-ups and sit-ups. I was there about one week before being moved to Basic Training at Fort Dix, New Jersey.

I had two Drill Sergeants in Basic Training: one man was tall, mustachioed, and white, while the other was short, slightly mustacioed, and black. I believe both of them were probably in their late thirties or so. The Little Black Drill Sergeant was around us most of the time, while the Tall White Drill Sergeant (forgotten their names) was doing office work. There were forty- four men in my unit in Basic Training.

The very first day of Basic Training, I got so nervous that I went to the Tall White Drill Sergeant's office and teared up, saying that I had made a mistake in joining and I wanted out. I felt stupid and was soon given a speech about how "he had forty-four men in his unit, and that he expected there were forty-four winners!" I went back to the unit and for the next nine weeks I gave this training my all. I gave 120% effort, inspired by his words. I remember having to change my glasses to Ugly Army Regulation prescription glasses.

In fact, by the end of Basic Training, we were about to go out to graduate, when the Short Black Drill Sergeant spoke to us all, giving us another pep talk about our future.

In his speech, he stated that while I did mess up more than most during that time, I gave more than 100% effort and I tried harder than anyone. He said I had given it a 120%-plus effort! I was pretty proud of myself and could not believe that, with all of us graduating and him speaking to us for the last time in our lives, that he chose to speak about the hard work that I had produced during that time in Basic Training.

CHAPTER 33

I was truly relieved to be finished with Basic and ready to get to my Advanced Individual Training (AIT for short) in Fort Sill, Oklahoma. While standing at attention for four hours and having shown our training with our "Rifle" (as the old saying goes, "This [pointing at our member] is your gun you use for fun, and this [my M16] is your rifle you use to shoot"), I couldn't wait to go home on Leave before heading back to the U.S. Army at Fort Sill, Oklahoma, for my AIT or Advanced Individual Training.

We were told at the barracks before going to graduation not to lock our knees when standing at attention. One guy passed out for locking his knees! During the graduation ceremony, I received my Army Service ribbon, my M16 Rifle medal, and my Grenade medal. I had a problem obtaining that Grenade medal. When the Private threw me the grenade, he threw it too fast. The fake grenade went off, and I thought I was almost deaf on one side. And I was yelled at, instead of the Private who caused the problem in the first place. That, frankly, was how my luck came and went while I was serving in Basic Training.

When I returned to Syracuse, I visited many family

members and friends, including the Recruiting Sergeant who signed me up for the U.S. Army and my best friend, Tony Callipari.

My next destination was Fort Sill, Oklahoma, home of the U.S. Army Premier Artillery Training Center on the East Coast. It was also where I would be stationed for my Permanent Party Station. To say that I was nervous was an understatement.

Being in a Permanent Party Station while an official U.S. Army Regular Active Soldier was much more relaxed than the training in Basic and AIT. The training program lasted twenty-four weeks.

There was a Private First-Class Falor in AIT and now my Permanent Party Station who was a nasty piece of work. My Father said to me, "There's always one asshole in the bunch!"

He sadly was right.

CHAPTER 34

This PFC Falor was verbally and sometimes physically assaulting toward me. He was either verbally abusive on a daily basis, or he looked at me the wrong way. This guy was a total jerk and the catalyst for my eventually getting out of the U.S. Army.

I'll never forget the day he tried to strangle me. Of course, I had my back toward him when he decided to grab a hold of my neck and try choking me. Luckily, I got free and used some obscenities as guys he knew watched and cheered him on.

When I tried to tell the Sergeants about these assaults, I realized I wasn't getting help. It wasn't until after coming back from being AWOL that I spoke to the Captain and they finally did something about it. Too little, too late.

The Captain threatened that anyone involved in attempting such actions would lose rank, as well as receive an Article 15. I told the Captain that I tried telling those above me, but never got help. It was amazing that I had to leave the unit before they finally did a damn thing about this group of ruffians.

Well, as the military goes, there was routine, and more routine, on a daily basis.

One particular week in the spring of 1986 (after becoming a Believer) I had not slept well at all. I may have gotten two hours each night. By the weekend, I was having mental issues with plenty of stress, not to mention the idiot PFC Falor causing problems. Two mechanics in my unit invited me to Church so they could speak with me about my soul destination. The following is what happened when I went one Sunday.

CHAPTER 35

"**H**ey, do you know where your soul will be when you die?" the mechanic asked me.

"Well, I don't know for sure, but I would like to know!" I told him, as I truly did want to know and had just been asking the Lord God that very question this week.

"Well, it's quite simple. Are you ready for the Truth?" he asked.

"Yeah, I've been waiting all my life for it!" I said.

So, there, at about 9 a.m. on April 27, 1986, at this man's church, Cameron Baptist Church, I was given the answer I had been waiting for all my life.

"Do you believe that Christ Jesus was God?" he asked me.

"Why, of course I do."

"Well, then," he said as he carried on, "the Truth is that Christ Jesus died for your sins, was buried, and rose again the third day! Do you believe this Gospel, Michael?" he asked.

"Yes, I do," I announced.

This lowly mechanic in my unit at Fort Sill, Oklahoma, had started something with his message to me. And he had no understanding of the depth, length, and height that this Good News would contribute to my life and to that of thousands around me. It would totally alter the course of my entire life.

Well, I will never forget the night I went AWOL (Absent Without Leave) from the military. I was in the mess hall eating my dinner when this PFC Falor and his entourage of evil cohorts decided to come up to me and squealed, "Hey Melice...you never know if you're going to wake up with your throat cut?!" And they all began to laugh.

After saying that, one of them showed me a four- inch blade, carefully out of view of any Sergeants.

The blade was three inches over regulation. Not only did they just threaten my life, but had a weapon to do so. They ended up getting Article 15s when I later told the Captain what they showed me.

I got nowhere trying to get help from any Sergeants above me in my unit, and so I decided to take off that evening. This was the advent of my leaving the US Army known as AWOL. I ended up eating very little after this confrontation and decided to head over to my favorite place to be alone: The Recreation Room, which held board games, books, art supplies, clay, etc.

I signed in, just as you were supposed to do.

They wanted to know where you were at all times, but this night would be different. I spoke kindly to the Rec Hall Supervisor (a female) and asked her if the road out front led out of this base.

"Why of course," she said. "Just turn right out of the door and go straight!"

I thanked her, went out the door, and began walking briskly. No one paid much attention to me as I walked down the road. I was simply in a pair of civilian jeans, a long sleeve light shirt (it was spring), and a good pair of sneakers.

I headed to Los Angeles, California.

CHAPTER 36

As I was walking that evening, all kinds of thoughts raced through my head.

What was I, nuts? I am going to get caught before I set foot off this base. Someone is going to think I am lost. Am I going to get Leavenworth Prison for this?

Where am I going? How am I going to survive leaving the military with hardly no money to my name?

I actually was quite frightened of the consequences of my actions, but soon got over all this as the weather that evening started to become chilly. I was now walking on the side of the highway, and every now and then I would look back to see if the Army had any MP's coming after me. This was a constant thought throughout my being AWOL. Though they probably wouldn't find out until the next morning at roll call.

Well, I had quite the adventure of walking, and hitching a few rides, to my destination, which was the next big city—a total of 110 miles to Oklahoma City.

My plan was to go to a Key Bank and have my mother wire me some money. She would simply think I was on base somewhere and would do this for me. I was confident my mom would do this for me.

As I was headed along the main highway, a man who was driving to an area diner offered me a ride there.

After I got a glass of water from the waitress, I began to survey the environment around me. Families were at tables eating, while single folks sat at the counter eating their food. I tried to look like I was really enjoying that water, but the waitress came over and asked me, "Sir, don't you want any food?" I said no and sort of slowly placed my head down. I thanked her, "Thank you anyway, ma'am."

A family eating a big chicken dinner not far from me was kitty-corner to my table. They had two adorable little girls at their table, and I couldn't help looking at the youngest little girl. She saw me, stared some, and then the other child, an older girl, went over to her mother and pointed at me, saying in a whisper, "Momma, that man doesn't have any food." Before I knew it, that family had bought me a chicken dinner. I looked over at them, waved, and said, "Thank you so very much!"

They yelled back, "Not to worry! You just enjoy! God bless you!" And I knew from this sweet gesture that they were probably Southern Baptists, being that I was in the Bible Belt west of the Mississippi River.

There were plenty of nice Christian folks in that area.

I finished my meal and thanked the waitress, telling her again to please thank that family for me. Imagine that? Some family doesn't know you, see you without food, and buys you a meal!

I teared up some in the restroom after finishing my meal. I was tired and overwhelmed with the circumstances that I had caused in my own life.

I actually thought I ruined what up to this point was a good start to my life. I walked back outside of the diner, where the weather was cooler and it was getting dark. A nearby owl said, "Who, Who?!"

I decided that I needed to rest along the side of the highway. And so, I lay down in the grass and tried to relax, continually aware that I was "Absent Without Leave," and had to be careful not to be seen by law enforcement.

I awoke the next morning (I think it was a Friday) with the sunshine shining in my eyes. Then I realized, as I felt the grass under my ass and some soreness in my back, that cars were driving by me at very high speeds. I needed to get up and get a move on. I was on the side of the highway.

CHAPTER 37

Well, I needed to get some money, because my plan was to go see California. I was now in Oklahoma City seven years before the bombing of the downtown federal building.

It was there, downtown, that I found a Key Bank, which was the bank where I had an account back in Syracuse. I walked in and soon found myself waiting next to an older couple who were waiting to talk to someone about a loan, I believe. I spoke to them both a while before they were called to speak to the loan officer. I had to call my mother and let her speak to this Key Bank to verify that I was who I was before getting money out of my account.

"Mom, I need to have $350 dollars wired to this Key Bank branch," I told her.

She started wondering why she had to do it, and I politely asked her to please just do it and assured her that everything was alright. Even though I was Absent Without Authorization from my Platoon Unit in Fort Sill. Thankfully, my mother gave the branch what they needed and said it would take about thirty to forty-five minutes to wire it across.

As I waited, I began again to speak to this lovely older couple who sat next to me. I explained to them I was waiting for money to go out west to California. They wanted to know if I had a place to stay overnight while I waited for the money.

"No, I haven't," I said, but I reassured them that I'd be fine.

"Don't you fret none, young man, my husband and I will get you a place to stay tonight," this older woman exclaimed to me. They smiled as they looked at me.

"That's alright, Ma'am, I'll be fine," I replied back to them both. The old man, who was wearing a hat just like his wife, piped up and said, "Nothing doing, young man, we would be happy to do it, it's no problem."

"Why, thank you so much! That's awfully kind of you!" I said back to them. When things like this happen, it still gives you hope that humanity isn't all that bad, if there are still some folks like this in the world.

As soon as we were all done with our business, I walked out of the bank with them and into their seventies Cadillac, which was in really good condition.

They drove me to a small motel, paid for the room, and said they would be back with something to eat.

CHAPTER 38

So, there I was in this small room with a bed, bathroom, chair, TV, and small table. I was AWOL from my Permanent Party Station, eighteen years old, and I had $350 dollars to my name, along with the clothes on my back. I sat down on the bed and started to cry. I felt quite lost, and though I was not a True Believer in Jesus Christ (brought up in the false doctrines of Catholicism), I began to pray aloud to the Lord.

I had talked to Him about how wrong I was, for leaving the Army and how I had placed myself into what seemed like such dire straits. I truly needed His help. What happened next was truly amazing. I heard a knock on the door of my room.

"Hello, we're back, Michael," I heard the old woman say.

"Be right there, ma'am." I walked to the door swiftly and unlocked it, letting them in the room.

They came in with such joy. I had no idea what they were bringing back to my room, but they were quite generous saints!

The old lady (sadly, I can't recall their names. Funny how we recall the bad events and names in our lives, but try recalling all the names of those who were good to you along the way?) was carrying two bags of groceries: bologna and cheese, tuna fish, and peanut butter and jelly sandwiches; all kinds of fruit, chips, milk, candy etc. I was overwhelmed at the sincerity and kindness that this older couple showed me. I told them that I would pay it forward one day by helping others the same way that they had helped me. I hugged and kissed them both saying, "This is truly wonderful what you have both done for me," (pausing) "I don't know what to say except for: Thank you for everything!"

They also had something else for me, in addition to the room, food, and drink. They had another bag from Sears; they had bought me a brand-new tape recorder (they play cassette tapes).

Frankly, I still have that tape recorder, and it still works being over thirty-two years later. It's amazing to think something bought in 1986 still works well today. They also gave me a bunch of cassettes tapes.

They said their good-byes and were soon out the door, never to see these gracious strangers again— except in Heaven one day? I looked around at what they had given me, and again began tearing up on the bed, thanking the Lord for such a blessing from these folks. I would only hope that the Lord blessed them for such lovely treatment they gave me.

Eventually, I began to eat some of the food, and I put

the rest in the refrigerator. I popped one of the tapes into the machine and pushed play. Listening to this tape, I discovered they were Bible messages that the older man (I found out he was some kind of reverend) had preached from the pulpit. They were a retired Christian couple from the area.

After eating some food, listening to some of the tapes, and watching a little TV, I decided to go to bed, as I had a long day the next day on a Greyhound bus headed for Los Angeles. I didn't sleep well, thinking about my current situation.

Amazingly, I was missing from my unit for thirteen days without any police tracking me down. That entire time I was missing, I kept looking over my back (I could hear my Aunt Rosie's voice in my head saying, "Watch your back, Michael!"), thinking any moment that the Military Police (MP) would catch and handcuff me; but this never happened. I was gone from my Unit nearly two weeks, I had written $700 dollars of bad checks, and had lied to my wonderful mother Angela Marie. I ended up paying back double that money with interest and fees, as well as receiving some other punishment for leaving my unit. I wonder what would have happened if I had never returned to the Army. Was there some statute of limitations on returning to your unit, being AWOL???!

CHAPTER 39

The next morning, I was going to be taking a bus out West to California. By the time I got to the bus stop, there were a few other folks also waiting.

Taking a Greyhound back in May 1986 was interesting, since there were only a few other folks on that bus. It was nice to have full roam of the bus without bothering anyone. I struck up a conversation with two young guys around my age. They had come together and were heading to Albuquerque, New Mexico.

While traveling west, we saw mainly hills and valleys along a desert highway, with some high boulders and stones that went on for miles.

When we got to our first stop in Albuquerque, there were four people remaining on the bus. Three of them got off, including the two young guys I had spoken with, and a young woman who was by herself.

We had a fifteen-minute stop, so I got off with the two young guys. They had a huge marijuana cigarette that they were going to share with me, so we found an alley. I only took two hits off this "joint," and I was feeling high. I think it was what was referred to as "Colombian" marijuana. Back in my day, you usually ran across four types of pot: Colombian, Hawaiian, Sensimilla, and home grown.

After a bathroom stop, I got back on the bus, thanking them and wishing them the best of luck in their lives.

As we drove from New Mexico to California, there was only the bus driver, one other man, and me on the bus. I was looking forward to getting to Los Angeles, as all my life I had wanted to go see this "famous" city, home of Hollywood. As the bus got closer, it was quite late at night. It was almost 11:30 p.m. when we arrived at the Greyhound station.

The second I steeped off the bus, I asked a worker unloading the luggage, "How do I get to the famous iconic Hollywood sign?"

I had finally arrived. Home of the so-called "Stars" and Disneyland, to name a few. Strangely, no Californian could tell me where to find the most Famous Iconic Sign in the World. I knew it was in the Hollywood Hills, but it's strange I never saw it.

PHOTOS

My father's parents, Nunzio & Palma Melice

Market Brings Out Harvest of Smiles

By JAMES EHMANN

Free balloons. Sunshine. Cheap peaches. Fresh flowers. All sorts of people — especially friendly people.

Tom Guerdon, one of the vendors, is all but sold out by 11:45 a.m. "This is a dynamite market for strawberries," he says. Most folks paid $2 a quart.

Guerdon has saved the last basket for one of last year's regulars, an older man on crutches. The old man spills little more than a dollar in change on Guerdon's table and reaches deep in a pocket for more.

"No, no," the vendor says. "That's enough." He takes the old man's shopping bag from a pin on one crutch and puts the strawberries inside.

Behind a nearby stand at the Tuesday Farmers' Market, old-timer "Spike Logan" strips the outer leaves from heads of lettuce. "I always clean everything up for the people," he says.

Logan, christened Dominick A. Logana 74 years ago, likes the people a lot. This boxer of long-ago fame was once a contender for the light-weight championship of the world, but his mother preferred he pursue a career in farming.

He did, and he is not sorry. Fifty years ago he carried his produce in a horse-drawn wagon to the downtown farmers' market on Fulton Street.

"We had crowds then like you wouldn't believe," said Pat Visconti, a produce dealer and long-time friend of Logan. "We'd have 250 or 300 hucksters buying vegetables and selling them door-to-door. You know how many you've got now?" he asks. "Two."

The dearth of hucksters at the modern market makes for no dearth of people, however.

tral New Yorkers stroll through the first Tuesday market of the season.

Most of 50 or so vendors deal in traditional farm produce. Many, like Mary Anne Kohutanich, sell marigolds, impatiens, yellow and red petunias. Some wares are more exotic. When Barb Kinney's homemade cranberry marmalade and blueberry jam sell out, she hypes less traditional jams — crabapple, orange gel, hot pepper.

The people have come for bargains and ensured freshness to be sure, but there is another draw to the outdoor mart. The crowd there is unlike crowds elsewhere, and few observers fail to notice the distinction.

Nearly everybody is smiling.

The vendors are smiling. The customers are smiling. The WCNY Teleuc volunteers handing out free balloons are smiling. No doubt Federal Building employees watching freed balloons blow by are smiling. The mounted policemen are smiling. The entertainers are smiling.

"What you'll be seeing," announces Roberta Wackett of the group Thornden Morris, "are a series of pre-Christian, English fertility and good-harvest dances. We'll start with 'Six Up for Highland Mary,'" she says.

A couple of smiling hard-hats have brown-bagged it. They lean against a fence in the market lot at Warren and Clinton Streets and eat, watching the show.

Others splurge. "I buy my lunch here every Tuesday," says Glen Lewis, who works downtown, "and I always save an item or two off my shopping list to get here."

The lunch offerings include German hot dogs, shrimp rolls, calzones, strawberry and banana smoo...

"Spike Logan" has been bringing fresh produce to the downtown Farmers' Market for 50 years. Logan, 74, likes the people a lot.

My Uncle Spike Logan Record Holder of
73 Year Syracuse Farmer's Market Farmer

Angela Marie & Dominick Samuel Melice
My parents wedding day July 20, 1963

My former step brother "Little Rock" and his ex-girlfriend Beth at my former house at 231 Hier Ave., Syracuse, NY

Personal Art Created by Cartoonist Dick Hodgins, Jr. for me.

Here's me(Michael Melice)Age:13.
Running at Corcoran High School
for a race against all the city's
Jr. High,andHigh Schools.We ran 2
miles.I'm shown here running
up a hill(steep).I was on Cross
Country team.My time:14:05 11/20/80

Myself running on 7th Grade Cross Country
Team for Grant Jr. High School

My godparents Mazie & Sylvester
Durandetti giving me my 1st rifle

My Grandma & Grandfather Procoppio
at my First Home in Fayetteville, NY.

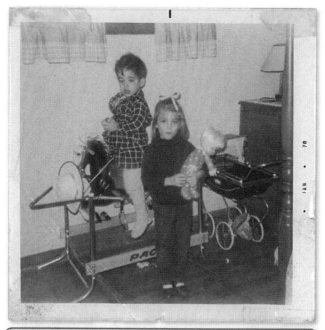

*My Sister Melissa (5 yrs old) and Myself
(3 years old) during 1970 Christmas*

*Myself (12 yrs old) and Teddy Catalano
before "Lemoyne Dolphins" Football practice*

During my 3rd Birthday. Cousin Mary Jo
Logan, Myself and my Sister Melissa

Easter Sunday 1969 Father Dominick
Samuel holding myself and Sister Melissa

Myself and 1st ex-wife Maria Dee Roberts
First Date walking at Erie Canal, NY

Connie Novak my dance instructor and
Myself during Christmas time 2005

Uncle Frank Logan, My Great Grandfather
on my Mother's side, Uncle Spike Logan

Friends Dan Ryan, Tony Callipari
and Myself (16 yrs old)

My Father's side of the Family
Back row (L to R) Cousin James King, Myself (glasses), my Brother Christopher and Cousin Chris Joyce. Next Row (L to R) Cousin Roberta Ayres, Cousin Doreen King, Uncle Bob, Aunt Dolly, Cousin Charleen Ferko, Cousin Mary Dawn Joyce, father Dominick (bent knees). Next Row (L to R) standing in front of Uncle Bob: Cousin Amy(Roberta's daughter), Cousin Miranda(Mary Dawn's daughter). Kneeling front (L to R) my Sister Melissa and her son my Nephew Dana Christian and Cousin Jeremy King (ball in hand).

Bible Teacher Gary Ingison, Linklaen Bible Church, near DeRuyter, NY. Taught me Right Division in the King James Holy Bible

In Front of 231 Hier Ave, Syracuse, NY
Myself (16 yrs),
Father Dominick (44 yrs),
Brother Christopher (11 yrs)

My Best Friend in New York: Antonio Callipari

231 Hier Ave, Syracuse, NY home with Mother and Stepfather Rocco J. Manzi, Jr.

6940 Highbridge Road, Lot 27, Fayetteville, NY My very first home I owned w/ my 1990 Mercury Cougar

Myself at my 1985 Henninger Senior Prom
I was 17 years old here

My Beautiful Date, Cristy Brown at Senior Prom

CHAPTER 40

Even though I write this story several years after it happened; I still have very vivid thoughts of that journey. Frankly, as I stepped off the Greyhound bus and looked at Los Angeles, I was apprehensive, due to being a deserter of the U.S. Army; and excited, because I was in an area that in the eighteen years of my short life I had never encountered, but had heard about and saw in the movies in all my years growing up.

I was AWOL for thirteen days. I was almost 1,300 miles away from where my job actually was, and in real trouble. In the back of mind, I kept thinking I was going to be caught and brought to United States Penitentiary, Leavenworth.

Leavenworth was (past tense) a maximum, high security prison that recently was brought down to a medium security prison for male inmates. I believe that it resides within a military base. Anyway, I thought I'd be breaking up large rocks into small rocks. Thankfully, that never happened.

Breaking up rocks sounds like the stories one hears about the ancient chain gangs. Chained together at the ankles, the prisoners worked on railroad tracks, landscaping, or roads. This mainly happened in the southern United States and had been phased out as of 1955, but evidently it was reintroduced back into Alabama in 2000.

But I am getting ahead of myself. I digress…

I really didn't have a lot of money, and so I couldn't rent a room. I was really hungry and so I decided to go to Little Mexico and grab a few authentic Mexican tacos. I figured I could find an authentic Mexican restaurant where I could get something to fill me up. Not only did I find a great little restaurant run by genuine Mexicans, but I also was in the presence of some very beautiful Spanish, Mexican, and Puerto Rican women.

CHAPTER 41

I walked into this really wonderful little Mexican restaurant, which was decorated like Mexico. A family of authentic, hard-working Mexicans ran it. One of the beautiful Mexican daughters served me. I could see that the father, who was in back cooking, was keeping his eyes on this "gringo."

It's just like in the movies, where some American walks into a Mexican restaurant and is watched carefully by the men of the family, who speak to their wives and daughters in their native tongue so you don't understand what they are saying.

This happens many times when waiting for food in Asian restaurants as well.

This is one of the reasons why in America there is division! Racism always divides! It's too bad we have been fed a heavy diet of racism in America! I think it's purposely done to divide the masses, so we would fight and kill each other.

Yes, I am a conspiracy person who believes in many conspiracies that are NOT just THEORY. Examples of

Conspiracies are: Assassination of President John F. Kennedy; 911 known as September 11th; The Northwoods Documents; the US School System's delibertate dumbing down of students (see Charlotte Iserbyt's book, *"The Deliberate Dumbing Down of America."*) One day the Truth will come out, and when it does, those around me who thought I was nuts will see the Truth for what it is: certain accuracy of the facts kept hidden all our lives!!

I enjoyed the two tacos I bought and decided to buy two more.

"Hello, Miss, can I get two more beef tacos, please?" I asked, enjoying my time of speaking to this beautiful young woman.

"No, problem, sir," she shouted as she quickly looked back at me and then conveyed to her father "in the Mexican language" my order of two more beef tacos.

While I was eating them, I spoke to her, and constantly looked up to see if her father or brothers were staring at me. The Mexican father had a look on his face that clearly stated I should stay clear of his daughter, and I was uncomfortable.

Before leaving the restaurant, I asked for directions to the famous Iconic Hollywood Sign in the Hollywood Hills, but she didn't know.

It was past midnight and quite dark. I used the restroom and then walked out, thanking them for the wonderful food, making sure to smile at the young woman. Her smile truly made my day.

CHAPTER 42

There I was on the streets of Hollywood, California, a deserter in the U.S. Army. It was past midnight and I had no place to sleep that first evening in Los Angeles. In the thirteen days I was away from the Army, I had maybe two nights of sleep in any shelter; the other eleven nights I slept on the street like a homeless bum.

There were a few times the police asked me to get up and go home. I did not argue. I simply walked elsewhere and found another bench. There were benches everywhere.

Los Angeles to me had a very bad city vibe. It was a beautiful metropolitan area, but like Washington, D.C., also had a feeling of a "sleazy" and evil environment.

Though the weather was nice, especially for those of us who lived on the East Coast. Here we were in February, and the temperature was a spring-like mid- eighties. In the evening it was 72 degrees, with a light breeze.

One place I had always wanted to see was the Hollywood Food Market, as well as a store that sold authentic autographed photos of Hollywood actresses and actors. The market had almost everything!

It covered an entire city block squared and was open on all sides, beneath a huge roof. It was the most massive outdoor food market I had ever seen. I was like a child in a candy store, seeing all the different kinds of ethnic foods, along with fruits and vegetables. It seemed like a good hundred vendors were selling their goods.

I had left this market having bought the following for $10 dollars:

- 1 pound of grapes 1 pound of ham
- 1/2 pound of cheese 1 loaf of French bread
- One four-pack of cheese Danishes 1 quart of skim milk

Imagine all that food for around $10 dollars in 1986. Why, back in those days you could rent a one-bedroom apartment in Los Angeles for around $350 dollars.

I found a park bench and started enjoying a sandwich of ham and cheese, and I ate some grapes. I was very hungry. I also enjoyed the Danish with milk. When I was finished with my meal, I chucked the bag into a waste basket. It was past dinner time when I finished eating, and again had to find a place to sleep for the night.

I wasn't proud at all that I had deserted the Army, though in the back of mind I didn't feel I had much of a choice. My Sergeants weren't listening; I had a job to do; and there was constant harassment as nobody heard me calling for Help!

Frankly, I saw things weren't going to change.

Amazingly, when all was said and done, the Captain of my platoon—or rather company—finally realized (after getting back to my Unit from being AWOL) that there was bullying and threatening against me. Sadly I had to commit a crime to get someone to notice. Unfortunately, I realized that I needed to get out of Dodge; and away from the troublemakers who weren't going to stop. It took me going AWOL to get the Army to do their job.

I tried in vain to find the famous Hollywood sign, but nobody could point out where it was. I was kind of mad about never finding it before leaving California.

CHAPTER 43

I did see some things in the Hollywood area that were famous, including the Chinese Mann Theater on Hollywood Boulevard, as well as Capitol Records, the Hollywood Walk of Fame, the Hollywood Museum, the Santa Monica Strip or Boardwalk (what I called it), Hollywood Bowl, Roosevelt Hotel, etc.

I saw the famous foot and handprints around the Chinese Mann Theater then walked across the street to the Roosevelt Hotel. I always wanted to go into the Roosevelt Hotel, and so I walked into the lobby.

What I didn't realize I would see upon walking into the Roosevelt Hotel was the heavy metal band Judas Priest, which was filming a music video in the lobby. They were all dressed in white suits, along with some good-looking models. The women in white were all talking around a table with wine, cheese, and fruit. They were models, no doubt.

I really don't recall all that I said to the singer Rob Hartford and guitarist K. K. Downey, but I did get their autographs on a Hollywood map. The one thing I told them was the clear Gospel of Salvation!

I had that Hollywood map for twenty years, when I eventually sold it for $20. After about an hour, I had to leave because they were still filming their music video. Years later I saw that music video on MTV.

I was clearly NOT a fan of Judas Priest, because I didn't like the music; but also because of the meaning of the name of the band: Judas (Betrayer of Christ), who had sold him out for thirty pieces of silver; and Priest, which is not necessary to have between you and the Lord unless you are in some false religion like Catholicism. So their name means: A Betrayer and False Mediator of God!

I truly didn't have enough money to get a room, and frankly I was getting a little horny in this big city known for Sex, Drugs, and Rock and Roll. No doubt, the so called "bad vibe" I had felt was probably part of the reason why I was having this feeling. Of course, it was the Old Sin Nature, but I definitely picked up on a feeling that was not good.

I decided to look around the streets of Hollywood for some female prostitutes, merely for a blowjob.

What I am about to explain isn't anything to brag about, but I simply wanted to add it because it shortened my trip and got me back to my military unit sooner than I expected.

What I found on the street, that evening at 7 p.m., were two women who were interested in conning me out of some money. I figured this out some years later, when I reflected on the streets of Hollywood, California.

CHAPTER 44

The first prostitute, a short black woman, took me for $20 and a lousy attempt at satisfaction. I saw a second black prostitute shortly after the first. She was in an alley, waving at me to come to her.

"Come here, sugar, you want something that's really good?" she asked me.

"Yeah, do you know how to give a good blowjob?" I asked her quietly, as I didn't want anyone to hear me.

"Why, sure I do, honey! I will give you the best you ever had!" she exclaimed, as she told me to lie down and let her do all the work. "Are you ready, sugar?" she asked.

"Yes, I'm as ready as I ever will be!" I said as I took a deep breath and she began her "work."

Well, she definitely didn't lie and left quickly after finishing with me. When I got up and straightened out, I found a hundred-dollar bill missing from my pocket. And both hookers were long gone.

Another thing I am ashamed to talk about was what happened next, as I was walking to Beverly Hills. I had always wanted to see the Beverly Hills Hotel.

I was walking down some street when I saw it. Right in front of this famous iconic place was a valet parking pole with tons of keys inside it. The Asians who guarded it were gone, and the keys were totally exposed. I wasn't truly thinking when I grabbed the first key within reach, looked in the doorway of the hotel, and not seeing anyone dashed quickly across the street into a parking garage.

CHAPTER 45

The parking garage had four levels, and I ran to the second level, hiding behind a vehicle in the corner, hoping that the person driving the car whose keys I had wasn't going anywhere anytime soon. I was scared out of my mind. When I took the key, I felt like I was playing out subconscious thoughts I had had as a teenager in wanting to steal a car. But never in my conscious mind did I think I would actually do such a deed.

But there I was, crouching on the ground in California, having deserted the Army; having stolen a key from a valet parking pole.

I stared down at this key in my hand. A card was attached to it, which said "White." I crouched on the ground for two full hours before I decided it was safe to get up and come out. It was 1 a.m.

While on the ground, I did hear the Los Angeles Police. I got up from where I was crouching and looked over the side of the parking garage. I was two stories up and from that perch I could see the front of the Asian Restaurant. There on front of the sidewalk was a beautiful white Mercedes Series 300E.

I walked out of the garage, looking all around, and I walked to the car. I was just about to commit grand theft auto.

I slowly pushed the key into this gorgeous white four-door sedan and turned it on. It clicked, and I found myself slowly moving into the seat of this luxury car, thinking to myself, "What am I doing?"

There I was on Sunset Boulevard, driving a stolen Mercedes-Benz. A vehicle I actually had always wanted to drive, and never thought I would.

Mercedes-Benz were dream cars to most teens back in the eighties. What was I thinking? I wasn't thinking, pure and simple! The registration said a medical doctor owned it.

CHAPTER 46

I don't know why, but the first place I wanted to go was to Santa Monica Beach. I drove there, as it was on some major route (Route 110, I think), which had really gorgeous views on the ocean side. This stolen Mercedes became my mode of transportation for nine days. I even put gas in the car a few times. I actually put a "For Sale" sign on it, thinking somehow I was going to sell another person's car.

I had a few folks offer me money, but I told them it wasn't enough, until these two black guys, who were also driving a Mercedes sedan convertible (the one I was driving was a hardtop), offered to trade the one they had for the one I was driving.

Frankly, I just began talking to them, as they really liked the white Mercedes I was driving. They would eventually bring it back to Florida, clean it up at a swap shop, and resell it to someone who would pay for it in cash.

CHAPTER 47

My thoughts about these two guys was actually right, and yet I ended up spending nine days with them. I can't recall their names, and yet, amazingly, I recall being treated fairly! I found out soon enough what these two dudes were up to; and why they had kept the top down on their Mercedes convertible.

These two black men were not only thieves, but they were drug dealers from Florida. Here I was a deserter, and a car thief, hanging around with two drug dealers and car thieves from Florida. Talk about some kind of stupid!

They showed me their "loot" of crystal meth that was kept in a red felt bag. All $10,000 of it!

Before I turned myself into the Army, these guys gave me a pair of Calvin Klein jeans from the eighties (frankly, the nicest pair of jeans I have ever worn) and a nice long sleeve shirt.

They brought me to a hooker's home, we did some of their drugs (sad to say), which for me was a few lines of crystal meth (a really potent form of cocaine) and a few "hits" of Colombian marijuana. I actually went out on

Hollywood Boulevard to buy some pot because of feeling so "high" from the crystal meth, but never scored any.

Another thing I did with these two drug dealers was to take a drive to San Diego. They needed to go there to do some "business." We went to some bar and grill that had a dance floor. They ordered drinks and I even had a mixed drink.

I decided to go dance with a gorgeous blonde. We started to slow dance. Within moments Ginger (I don't recall her real name) and I were "Dirty Dancing." The movie did not come out for another year (in 1987), so I was making it up at that moment. My mother had once told me that she "dirty-danced" back in the fifties.

I will say one thing about Ginger: Not only was she incredibly good-looking, but she was quite the kisser. The sad fact was that these two dealers were ready to go, and I had to leave with them. I had been speaking to her some as we danced, and I had convinced her to go to a hotel room. This was something I always regretted. I believe she was better looking than Farrah Fawcett. Of course, beauty is in the eye of the beholder.

Ginger could have been a model. I would have a great memory of dirty dancing with her. I definitely understood why, years later, my friend David "Scott" Flanagan moved to this area.

My friend Tony told me some years ago that Scott had moved to California near San Diego and married a "witch."

When he said that word "witch," I thought he was being mean about her looks, and I said to him, "Oh, come on,

Tony! Don't be so mean about Scott's wife!"

"No, man," he said, "she's really a bona-fide white witch." He said Scott married her in some coven. Scott has a son with this woman, and I really wonder how his son will turn out.

Scott tried to tell me once on the phone that she was a good witch. I said to him, "Why would you call any witch good?" He and I didn't argue too long, and I gave him the Gospel, for which he said, "Well, hey, Mike, I'm glad that works for you my friend!"

At least I could say that he has no excuse with God: He heard a clear understanding of the Gospel Salvation. I haven't talked to him since. I wished the best for him and his family. I told him I would pray for him.

When we got back from San Diego (the two dealers and I), we visited some other drug dealer who they knew in Los Angeles. We all got into my stolen Mercedes and went over to some woman's house who was a prostitute!

These two hoods were trying to get into bed with this Puerto Rican hooker, but she wasn't having it.

She just wanted drugs. I think frankly she was just "teasing" them to get the drugs.

This is what I found out afterward when I spoke to them. I was waiting in the Mercedes with this third drug dealer we had picked up that night, who was a real "heavy-hitter" dealer. This guy dealt with wealthy folks, including celebrities.

This third drug dealer was with me, waiting in the

Mercedes. I think the two dealers I was with would have made a huge drug deal, but that never ended up happening.

I ended up telling this third drug dealer that I was AWOL from the U.S. Army and, all of a sudden, he opened the car door, slammed it shut, and started strolling away. The third drug dealer was a tall guy, and so his strides were really long, meaning he could get away in a hurry!

CHAPTER 48

So, I went into the house where these two drug dealers were and told them what just happened. They realized that they needed to get going as well. So we left, one in the driver's seat and the other in the passenger seat, while I sat in the back. We began to talk about me turning myself into the Hollywood Police Station to get back to the Army. I had been away for twelve days at that point.

Any longer, and I may have gotten into more serious trouble. I thanked them actually for helping me to survive some, for the clothes, and I opened the car door.

"You all take care of yourselves! Be careful! Life can be a trip, and you sometimes never know where you will end up!" I said to them. They waved to me as I headed up the stairs of the Hollywood Police Station, walking slowly. I knew I had a long journey ahead.

I walked into the station, saw a vending machine, and bought a Milky Way bar. I took a few bites and went up to the front desk. I told the police officer about being AWOL from Army, and he told me to sit down. I gave him all the information he needed to file the report, along with my Military I.D. card.

As I waited, I was placed into a small five-by- nine-foot, white, concrete prison cell. When I entered this little cement cell, there was a man who looked like he had stepped out of a cave. The police officer had taken the candy bar out of my hand and tossed it in the garbage bin. This type of treatment I received while I was processed back to my unit in the Army.

CHAPTER 49

Inside the holding cell, there was a man with a big afro; he looked to be of Spanish descent. He looked as though he had not cut his hair in years, and it was not only on his head, but he had a mustache and beard that were so thick you could not see the man's face. The hair on his back looked like it was an inch thick.

It was a hideous sight. He grunted at me a few times, and then he sat down in the right-hand corner. I stood up most of the time. I was somehow calm and scared at the same time, since I had no clue what was going to happen or when.

It felt like forever, being in this small concrete cell. Two hours passed before some police officer came for me and brought me to his desk. As I sat next to the desk, he told me that I had to wait for the Navy, which was coming to get me because they were closer than any Army base. So, I went back into the cell for another hour!

Finally, I heard the Naval MP's (Military Police) coming my way toward the jail cell. The door opened and I heard a voice yell, "Alright, come out, Soldier! Move it, move it!"

I knew that I was dealing with some naval personnel who cared not for my welfare, because he acted more like he was picking up sheep going back to its owner.

Of course, in the military you are considered government "property" of the United States. Then again, the United States is a corporation in reality, and we are merely pawns or serfs for the elite "owners" of this corporation!

CHAPTER 50

I was sent to the nearest naval base, which happened to be in San Diego. Frankly, because I was a criminal, they treated me like one. I was cooperating and I hated being questioned in such a harsh way. I gave them the info they wanted and did not act rudely.

The naval officer who questioned me was an asshole, first class! There was no need for him to be so rude, and I told him so. He barked at me and said something about me being a criminal of the U.S. Military and that he could treat me any way he saw fit.

And the fact is, the reason I left the U.S. Army is because someone in my own Army unit was making my daily life in the military a living hell. It's interesting how, when I got back, that they finally decided to do their job.

I found it really offensive to have to wait in some cell (there was no door, but steel bars like a prison door instead) on top of a dirty, pee-stained mattress that I was afraid to touch for fear of disease. I got off the mattress, and some guard came by and told me to get back on it. I kept my skin away from touching it, allowing only my clothing to make any contact. I could always wash my clothes!

I waited for what seemed like forever. I don't recall my thoughts, but I knew I had a lot of regret. I also was wondering what would happen to me when I got back. They finally brought me lunch.

This disgusting lunch consisted of a soggy sandwich, celery, carrot sticks (four of them), a small carton of milk, and a piece of sweet cake that tasted gross. It had too much sugar. I ate the veggies, took a bite of the sandwich, and drank half the milk.

Finally, the Army MPs (Military Police) came to get me. Placing me in handcuffs, they led me out to the Army MP vehicle. I got in the backseat, looking forward to getting back to my unit. I was another step closer to getting this ordeal over. What I truly needed was a shower, sleep, and good food.

When I arrived at the airport in Los Angeles, I was escorted by a Sergeant whose left hand was handcuffed to my right wrist. His dress greens were placed over our hands, covering it so it would not be embarrassing as I boarded the plane heading back to Fort Sill, Oklahoma.

It was very awkward to be handcuffed to this black Sergeant, and I had to remain this way for the entire trip. In the first ten minutes, he explained all that would happen when we landed. I tried to close my eyes and relax; I was more scared going back than I was when I deserted my Army unit.

There were a lot of guys in the unit who sure gave me quite the look of disgust. Honestly, I was thinking how good it would be to get the hell out of the Army after going through this.

I felt ashamed as I got out of the vehicle in handcuffs, waiting to be un-cuffed! I never would have done that again. It certainly didn't help my military career! My U.S. Army contract had almost one and a half years left on it and, sadly, I wanted originally to make it a twenty-year career!

CHAPTER 51

There was one more bad thing that happened to me. I have PFC Falor to blame for leaving the Army in the first place; and a second time for this incident that happened. I was in some bar on the strip (on the base of Fort Sill) when someone asked me if I wanted to buy a "joint": a marijuana cigarette. Sure, I said, and I paid him $5.

Well, I mentioned this incident to some guy in the unit I thought I could trust, and before I knew it, PFC Falor squealed on me to the Sergeants.

The sad fact is that there are "few" folks in the world you could totally trust. Just when you think you know someone, they turn on you.

This guy simply had it in for me, and until he was out of my life he was a monkey on my back.

The next thing I knew, the Army brought the "dogs" (makes me think of the song "Who Let the Dogs Out?!") into our barracks to shake down the place.

They ended up finding the "grass," which the officials said was no stronger than a potent form of oregano.

I was lied to, which ended up costing me a rank from E3

(just gotten the promotion) to E2. Although my rank was E2 when I got out of the service, always thought of myself as an E3. I found that the scumbag Private Palor had set me up to take the fall.

In fact, throughout every stage in my life I have had to deal with bullies. In elementary school there were a few. In junior high school there was Joe Greco, who had started bothering me in seventh grade (I ended up hitting him after a ninth-grade Social Studies exam; he got five-days' suspension, and I got one day). In high school there was Scott Travers, who was verbally abusive to me most of the four years I attended Henninger Senior High School. Known in the yearbook as "The Devil," Scott Travers was not a nice guy!

Also, in High School, there was a Greek guy, Sotiris Gotsis, who actually spat on me for no reason during lunch hour to see if I would hit him. I saw this guy on Facebook years later, mentioned the incident, and he said he doesn't remember. Give me a break!

Who would forget spitting on someone in twelfth grade?

All of these people were bullies in the meanest sense of the word. Even into my adulthood I have over the past thirty-plus years come across such lowlife scum.

The sad fact is that I believe over half of this Earth is filled with such people who simply want to make life difficult for others?! Why? For what purpose? As a Christian man I know mankind sins because of the Old Sin Nature in all of us.

"Wherefore, as by one-man sin entered into the world,

and death by sin; and so death passed upon all men, for that all have sinned." (Romans 5:12)

CHAPTER 52

After speaking to my Captain, First Lieutenant, and Sergeants about what had taken place that made me go AWOL, a company meeting took place. The Captain got up and he explained how serious an offence it would be for ANYONE who was physically or verbally abusive to his fellow Soldier. If I am not mistaken, I believe that if the threats were either verbal or physical, the Soldier would be kicked out of the Military!

Sadly, the guys in my unit who had caused the problem in the first place got no more than a slap on the wrist as far as I could see. So much for the power of these Captain's words. They simply had gotten an Article 15 court martial?

This only seemed to irritate PFC Falor and his cohorts. So that now I simply got "evil looks" from them. Imagine being in a military unit where you had to worry about those who were supposed to be fighting **with you,** instead of dealing with the real enemy you're supposed to be fighting **against!**

"Wherein in time past ye walked according to the course of this world, according to the prince of the power of the air, the spirit that now worketh in the children of disobedience."
                                                    (Ephesians 2:2)

The course of many in this world is along a one- way ticket to Hell, and many are heading on its broad highway!

My next meeting took place with a Lieutenant Colonel who, after explaining what had happened, gave me the following punishment:

- 14 days extra duty (which I completed)
- $300 fine (which I paid)
- $333 plane ticket from California I had to pay back (they took out of my next paycheck.)

And 30 days in a correctional facility that happened to be a few blocks away from my unit.

The day that I left for my thirty days was an awful day. Not only was I afraid of what would happen there, but also how I would be treated when I returned to my own Army unit.

It was a warm sunny day, that day I was driven over to the Army brig to complete "my time." It was literally a stone's throw away! The barracks were around the corner from it.

I stood at parade rest with my huge five-foot-tall Army knapsack in which I had packed my military clothes and toiletries. I stood there with this bag sitting next to me on the ground to my left. What happened next was the most grueling, and physically demanding, workouts that I had ever encountered since being in the military or anywhere!

I had to go through what they called "being processed" into this Army brig unit, which, as anything with the U.S. military, involved tons of paperwork and questions.

By the time I had gotten "processed" into this Army jail and to my barracks (there were two barracks for the inmates and two main buildings for staff), I had done the following workout in forty minutes! This is no lie or exaggeration.

- 500 push-ups
- 500 jumping jacks
- 300 sit-ups
- 500 squat thrusts

And beyond that, my military knapsack was tossed across the room, where my belongings scattered everywhere.

Soon I was in the barracks and unpacking my belongings into the floor foot lockers under my bed. I was out before I hit the pillow.

CHAPTER 53

Now I was in for another round of bullying. This time there was a guy in the military jail who for no reason didn't like me. Maybe because I was better looking, and in better shape than this bully? I really don't know. This is what I called "too stupid for words."

What a total idiot he was. Honestly, he was like the rest of the bullies whom I had dealt with in life: They all had a screw loose! He had several loose!

There was actually one good guy (forgot his name.) in the Brig who was considerate toward me.

Also, the Sergeants weren't too nice! In fact, I learned an awful lesson when I showed a photo of my ex-girlfriend (Cristy Brown), whom I had taken to my senior prom, that prompted another "workout." This really punished my body. Have you ever done forty-five minutes of almost straight continuous push-ups? I had to do it for showing a picture that I wasn't supposed to have.

Imagine going down for twenty push-ups, and then on the way getting back up, being dropped again for twenty more pushups, for an entire forty-five minutes. Again, I thought I was going to pass out or die!

This Sergeant was a female, real pretty don't yah know: A Puerto Rican woman who always dressed for P.T. (Physical Therapy) in seriously short shorts! You could see things that you weren't supposed to see when she wore them. I think this type of power over men was something she truly got off on.

Another aspect in this life that's very dangerous: A woman abusing her power she had over men. I think it's wrong PERIOD to use one's power abusively over anyone, but it happens all the time.

When I started looking like I was going to faint, she stopped ordering me down for push-ups.

"I suppose you are aware now, Private, of not having a photo on you here!," she said. "Don't you ever let me see that picture again, are you clear! Speak up, Private, I can't Hear You!" She shouted this to me, as I was so tired I could hardly grasp her words.

"Yes, Ma'am, Sergeant! Loud and Clear!" Off I went, never to show that photo to anyone. The embarrassing aspect of it all was that the other men in the unit simply gawked at me.

I was having a difficult time walking back to the barracks. The bully I mentioned said something like, "Well, I guess you met Josie?!" (I can't recall what her real name.) He said this grinning a big slick grin that begged me to hit the jerk. But I had trouble raising my arms after that "lesson" I had been taught by the female Sergeant. And besides, I also didn't need the trouble!

There was a simple but very full routine that took place in this jail, and every day for a month we had P.T. (Physical Training) twice a day! There was this obstacle course that we had to run through, and after the course was finished, we had to do so many push- ups, pull-ups, and sit-ups. Then we had a two-mile run with the Sergeants who enjoyed watching us do all that, ending with stretching. Then we were "marched" to the cafeteria for breakfast.

Every day we had to pick up cigarette butts in the yard, and then "shine mirrors" in the officer buildings so that when they looked into the mirror they could see a shine. Of course, we had weekly hair cuts, too, that we had to pay for even if we didn't want one.

It was one of the many "rules" we had to go by while we were "inmates." Interestingly enough, I still to this day keep my hair extra short. A habit it had become, and it sorts of suits me too! Less maintenance. I do a monthly "buzz" with an electric Wahl razor.

CHAPTER 54

By the time I was finished with my thirty days in the correctional facility, I had lost thirty pounds of fat and gained twenty pounds of muscle. I could do forty pull-ups, 500-plus push-ups; 400 sit-ups, straight through on both of them. I never looked so good in my life! If you ever wanted to be in shape, this was the place!

The last day of being in that correctional facility was a happy one. I was finally going back to my unit so I could focus on my job in the Army!

I recall the stares I got for coming back to my unit. There were some who were not happy to see me, and a faithful few friends who were glad I was finally done with my punishment. The other reason that they stared is that I was truly in great shape.

Again I was a target for bullies, because of my Totally Fit Body, and there were some jealous guys who were talking trash about it. Frankly, it was getting old. Some guys just NEVER grow up.

I recall that it wasn't that much longer after I had gotten back that the Sergeants took myself and a few other

Privates out for the night. Why they did this, I really don't remember. Maybe because they failed to do their job before I went AWOL and felt guilty? The first thing I recall is going to one of their homes and drinking a shot of tequila. One of the Sergeants drank "the worm" in his shot of tequila. I'd only heard about that before. Yuck.

CHAPTER 55

After we were done taking our shots, we went to the local strip mall in town where many soldiers went to drink, because it was a short distance from the base. I went into one of the bars with a few of the Sergeants and they bought we "privates" a round of beer. Frankly, their behavior this night toward me was really odd.

After half a beer, I told them I was going to wander over to the "strip joint" because I had not been there in a while.

While playing pool, I was being "coaxed" and flirted at by some of the women who actually flashed their crotches up to the pocket of the holes, trying to get me to miss the shot. I ended up talking two of the women into sleeping with me, but it ended pretty abruptly due to one of the woman's boyfriend, who found out and stopped it!

What ended up as a heated discussion began to make sense as to why it all was happening. Standing at one of the tables against the wall was that "bully" whom I had encountered in the Army brig, and an E4 Specialist, also from the brig, both of whom were scum.

I don't recall much of the conversation between him

and me, but I do remember that there was an E5 from the Army brig (who was one of the commanding NCOs there in charge) who was not only drunk, but grinning as well. Again, I had never done a damn thing to these men.

"Me, those guys at that table and those fifty soldiers against the wall are going to kick your ass, buddy!" this bully shouted over the loud music, and then walked back to the table.

"Whatever," I said as I looked against the wall and saw at least thirty guys, some of them pounding their fists into their other hands as an indication that they wanted to fight.

I started to pray that some Marines would walk in, when a few minutes later four Marines walked in with their dress blues. I thanked God for it! I walked up to one of them whom I knew. Usually Army and Marines don't associate with each other, but I always made it a point to be friendly to everyone.

Knowing a few of these Marines was a good thing.

I walked up to one of them and explained the situation. I asked them, "Do you all think you could escort me out here to the next bar where some friends of mine are?"

They agreed. "Sure, come on," one of them said, as they placed me in between the row of them, with two in the front, two in the rear, and me in the middle. When they got me next door, I turned to them and said, "Thanks a lot, gentleman!"

One of the drunk Sergeants turned to us and said, "What are THEY doing here?!"

I told them not to pay attention, as they were drinking too much. The Marines didn't seem to care. They simply turned around and headed back to the other place. Talk about luck!

CHAPTER 56

Well, I was back together with the Sergeants and Privates that I came with and told them I was taking a taxi back to the base. As I was walking out to the taxi, the Specialist and Sergeant emerged three doors down from where I was. They were looking at me angrily, and I was just glad to leave them in the rear view mirror.

When I got back in my unit, I was ready to get back to work. Years later, looking back as a veteran, I am glad that I got out of the U.S. Army when I did on 15 August 1986 exactly 1 year 1 day I served in the military! I might not be writing down these experiences, because I may have been killed in the Persian Gulf Wars. Well, the next thing that happened changed my entire life from that point up to the present time: The Salvation of my Soul!

"God is faithful, by whom ye were called unto the fellowship of his Son Jesus Christ our Lord."

(1 Corinthians 1:9)

CHAPTER 57

There was a man in my platoon unit of Company B who was not only one of our mechanics, but the Christian man who led me to Christ Jesus! Little does this man know how he truly affected my life in a very radical way. Thanks to him, I was set on the path of the Truth of Jesus Christ, which would lead me to the real promise of this life: To be eternally saved from Hell and one day be in the heavenly places with my Lord and Savior Jesus Christ!

"Who hath delivered us from the power of darkness, and hath translated us into the kingdom of his dear Son."
(Colossians 1:13)

I will never forget that moment, the day, that the mechanic came over to me and started asking me some questions about my spiritual destiny. I had waited all my life for this moment of truth. I had always wondered why nobody ever shared this marvelous knowledge with me?

That is the reason why I do all that I can to reach others to share this truth—from showing others the Gospel on the internet, passing out Gospel tracts, and verbally speaking the Truth to others whenever possible.

At the only high school reunion I went to (my twentieth-year reunion of Henninger High School), I was hoping I would have been able to get in front of the group with a microphone and give the clear representation of the Gospel and then leave. But it never happened.

I did individually share the salvation message to some of the former high school students. I found a few classmates who just happened to be believers. I was upset to learn that one person failed to come. Hope Wynkoop, whom I found out after high school had been raised a Christian. She told me on the phone. Sadly, though, she never in all the four years I knew her in school, and on the track and cross-country teams, did she ever give me this truth I so desperately needed.

"Who do you believe Jesus Christ is?" the mechanic in my Army unit had asked me.

"I believe He was and is God," I said.

"Yes, but He also died for your sins, was buried, and rose again" (found in 1 Corinthians 15:3,4 KJV). "Do you, Michael, believe this Good News, also called the Gospel?" he asked me.

YES, I did!

So, this was the moment for which I had waited my whole life of eighteen years? The previous week I had prayed to KNOW the truth of how to go to heaven.

He and another believer (both mechanics) who was beside him in the barracks looked on and smiled the biggest smiles I had ever seen.

I had now possessed eternal life with Christ in the heavenly places. April 27,1986, at 9:09 a.m. was the exact time that I stepped from death to life in the Salvation of my Soul! They both congratulated me and gave me a hug each.

I am sure that any soldier who saw or heard this exchange who didn't believe God's word thought we were crazy! The fact remains, it's the world that's crazy. One of my favorite all-time older movies was "It's a Mad, Mad, Mad, Mad World." If that movie doesn't show just how MAD this world truly is, then I don't know any more what to say to you.

"For the preaching of the cross is to them that perish foolishness; but unto us which are saved it is the power of God." (1 Corinthians 1:18 KJV)

CHAPTER 58

Imagine, knowing for the first time that when you die, your soul had been redeemed, paid for, and reconciled on its way to heaven either at the rapture or at your death, whichever came first!

I started to go to church with these two brothers in Lawton, Oklahoma, at Cameron Baptist Church.

I recall the very day when I was at this assembly to get baptized in water, even though some years later, in 1990, I learned I didn't need to get water baptized.

"For Christ sent me not to baptize, but to preach the gospel: not with wisdom of words, lest the cross of Christ should be made of none effect."

(1 Corinthians 1:17 KJV)

On the day I was water baptized, there was quite a big procession of folks (seemed like the majority were around my age, between eighteen and twenty-five years). We were several men and women walking toward these pillars with stairs leading down into a pool, which were hidden behind curtains when the church was in session. We had to wear these waterproof robes with our underwear underneath.

For a brief, quick moment, my robe opened some and, as I began to close it tighter around my body, I saw that a young woman noticed my underwear. She smiled and looked away with innocence.

After the whole process, I got dressed again and went out to the pews where I began singing an uplifting hymn with everyone else. The pastor at the assembly was named Bob Jones III, and he was a relative of Bob Jones, of Bob Jones University. He looked over at me and smiled. Years later, in 2018, I spoke to the assistant pastor at that time about what had happened to me. He actually remembered me!

"Who will have all men to be saved, and to come unto the **knowledge of the truth."**

(1 Timothy 2:4)

I remember speaking to Pastor Jones after the service. I had tears of joy in being a "new creature in Christ!" I recall after getting saved and redeemed that I had begun talking to everybody I possibly knew, as well as folks whom I didn't know. I was, as some would have say, "on fire for the LORD!"

Amazingly, I still to this day look forward to speaking to others about this soul-saving gospel. One time I had estimated just how many times I have given out the Gospel: Over 15,000 folks have heard the "Truth of the Gospel" from my lips!

"The fruit of the righteous is a tree of life; and he **that winneth souls is wise."**

(Proverbs 11:30)

Things started to look up, and I thought this is what I needed to change my life around.

Some years later, in the 1990s, I spoke to a man named Dr. Rivera, a former Italian Jesuit priest in the Vatican who left Catholicism and also got saved. This man helped Jack Chick to create a series of six comic books called "Alberto, Part One to Six." His English was not the best, but I spoke to him for about five minutes, and to his wife (who was also born in Italy but spoke better English) for a half hour. It wasn't much longer after I spoke to them that "they" murdered him. The "they" are part of the New World Order. They certainly did not want him speaking the truth about the Catholic church to the world and exposing their evils.

I also had the opportunity to give the Gospel of Jesus Christ to well-known TV Evangelist Pastor Joel Olsteen who could not give me this Good News from God's Word? There have been many other well-known men and women to whom I have given the Gospel (in 1Corinthians 15:3,4 KJV) over the years.

I just praise the Lord He gave me the opportunity, words, and courage to give it to them. Every week I give it out to <u>at least</u> three folks via phone, online, or in person.

CHAPTER 59

In the last week of May 1986 about a week before I had a mental breakdown was strange. I think I got less than ten hours of sleep the entire week. In a week, there are 167 hours. So, you could say with being in the U.S. Army Regular Active with about eight hours' sleep: I was working on pure adrenaline that entire week. Not a good thing, and I had set myself up for a breakdown. I called it a short circuit of my brain.

It was a nice Sunday, and I was on the church van with the few men who had led me to the Lord. We had gotten to the church, Cameron Baptist Church, and it was almost time to go to Bible study. I went in and sat down next to someone. I recall that as I entered, I felt something strange about my body. I had no idea what it was, but I would soon find out.

While speaking to a brother next to me, my body began to quiver and tears started to flow down my cheeks. I looked at the guy and said, "I'm going to lie down in the other room. I don't feel so good! I don't know why I am crying!?"

"Sure," he said. "Go ahead, brother."

So off I went into the other room, placing my King James Bible and notebook above me on a shelf as I lay down and tried to close my eyes.

A few minutes later I was in the middle of what felt like and looked like an epileptic attack: A mental breakdown. The best way to imagine it is to think of a computer hard drive crashing.

The people in the nearby room having Bible study heard my screams, and before I knew it they were rushing me to the base hospital. I don't recall much from that evening. I recall being strapped to a gurney and spoken to by several doctors, who told me that they were going to give me something to calm down.

"This won't hurt, Mr. Melice," said one of the doctors. "Just hold still the best that you can, and relax."

I could feel a slight prick (a needle) in my arm, and I began to drift off into a powerful sleep. I slept very well from whatever it was they gave me (I think it may have been thorazine), and actually had the best sleep in my life. The only time I slept that well, I believe, was when I was a baby. I was told by my mother, Angela Marie Manzi, that I slept better than my brother and sister.

"You were the best baby, and the best child growing up!" my mother once said to me.

When I awoke several hours later, it was early morning and my mouth felt dry.

"Nurse, help me, please. Somebody help me!" I yelled.

A nurse came walking very quickly into the room

and said, "What can I do for you, sir!?!"

I looked into her soft blue, beautiful eyes and said, "I really need some water, please? Could I get some, and maybe get out of these restraints?"

I recall she was brunette, and there's no other hair color on a woman that turns me on more than a black or brown hair color. She was a very attractive and gentle woman.

She came soon with a cup and pitcher of water. Having poured the water, she came over to me and, holding my head, placed the water to my mouth as I drank. I thanked her, and she said, "You're welcome. The doctor will be in shortly to get the restraints off you. I don't have the authority to do so."

"Thank you, ma'am, so much!" I said to her in a low, somewhat tired voice.

I could say one thing: I was treated very well as a patient in this hospital and the next hospital. The third and last hospital before getting discharged from the U.S. Army was not as attentive, but they really understood psychiatric patients better than any place I have ever been seen.

While watching a scene in the movie *Mr. Jones* with Actor Richard Gere (who grew up next to my cousins in North Syracuse, New York) some years later, I thought about the above scene. I really connected with Richard's character in that film. It didn't fully capture the actual life of someone with bipolar disorder, but it's the closest I have ever seen to helping someone understand a little of what I was dealing with in my own life.

After waiting for what seemed like forever, he finally

came. I heard a knock on the door and then the doctor appeared.

"Hello, I'm Doctor (blank, don't remember his name) and I just wanted to let you know that we will take off those restraints for you and place you in a regular hospital room today!"

"Good, I need to feel a little normal here. I need a good shower and shave!" I explained to him. "No problem, sir!" stated the doctor.

Before I knew it, I had taken a shower, was in a room of my own, and had shaved my face.

CHAPTER 59

Looking back on this ordeal, as vivid an experience it was, I recall a lot of routine in the hospital. I was first in the base hospital in Fort Sill, Oklahoma, where I was stationed. Then I moved to an Air Force hospital in Texas (I think it was called Lackland Air Force Base), before spending the remainder of my hospital stay at Brooke Army Medical Center (BAMC for short) in Fort Sam Houston, in San Antonio, Texas. Each time they transported me was via stretcher in a helicopter with other veteran patients.

I recall being put through a lot of psychological exams and being given medicine. At one point in my treatment, I literally lost my voice for three or four days due to some psychotropic drug I was taking. So, at this time when I wanted to talk to my mother on the phone, the nurses had to speak for me.

After my mental breakdown, I remember the doctor telling me that I was on Haldol. Let me tell you, when I found out years later just how powerful this drug was, it really floored me. You could have put an elephant to sleep with the power of this drug! Haldol, or Haloperidol, is an antipsychotic drug.

The moment that the doctors told me this, I had told them that I would find a way one day to get off medicine. If it was the last thing I would do in my life, I told them I would one day be drug free. It took nineteen years to reach this goal, but I wasn't going to fail this challenge. There was no way that I was going to be some damn zombie on Psychotropic drugs for the rest of my life.

The sad fact is that many veterans I knew back in the mid- to late eighties in the Syracuse VA, who were on Psych meds, are still currently on them.

Instead of believing they could be free of these harmful drugs and being brainwashed into thinking like so many others who follow their "doctors' orders," they chose in their own minds the lies instead of the truth. It was simple mind over matter. If you don't mind it won't matter, and vice versa.

It was the best thing that I could have done in the beginning of being diagnosed with a mental disorder. The term most folks use is mental illness. The problem is that most folks don't know that the term is actually an oxymoron. I won't get into any detail about this, but you can see the explanation in the book, *Psycho-heresy* by Martin and Deidre Bobgan. (I spoke to them once on the phone). The term "mental illness" is actually not medically accurate, but what is called a misnomer.

There was a point during my stay at the Fort Sill, Oklahoma, hospital that I noticed a little red light in the upper right-hand corner of the little mini television in my room. One of the male nurses told me that when that red light was on, the folks in the TV could actually see and hear me.

Can you imagine a nurse telling a mental patient on Psychotropic drugs that the people inside the TV could actually hear me? Talk about cruel and unusual punishment! These nurses who told me this were the "mental cases" as I saw it years later. They were the ones who I believed were sick in the head.

It's what started me to have hallucinations. For example, I thought the cast of the Waltons could hear me, and I thought they were raising money for me in one episode. I also was hallucinating so badly that I thought that I saw and heard Tinker Bell, Jiminy Cricket, and Mickey Mouse.

Another time I was forced to take a needle. They were giving me something to simply shut me up. Most of the nurses I had (females) were attractive and had beautiful smiles. It seemed like many of the male nurses had some bitter attitudes toward me.

Bullies…they seemed to be everywhere!

Army bases are like night and day compared to Air Force bases! The U.S. Air Force has civilian cooks; and everything is much newer and cleaner than any U.S. Army base!

I wouldn't be at this Air Force base very long, but I actually felt the safest there, and people listened to me more, than at any of the Army bases.

There were only six other psychiatric patients at the Air Force base with me, plus staff. I could not believe how incredibly gentle and sweet the staff of Lackland Air Force

Base were toward me. The other inpatients were quite genuine toward me, and very kind and helpful.

CHAPTER 61

I would soon placed at the last psychiatric hospital before being discharged from the military: Brooke Army Medical Center, or BAMC for short.

I would be there for eighty-eight days, which felt like forever. I would call my mother, begging her get the local Congressman to get me out. But my mother persuaded me from getting out too soon, knowing that if I had, I would have been in quite a mess. It's possible I would never have gotten my disability with the help of the Disabled American Veterans (DAV) in Syracuse, some five years after my discharge.

I underwent a huge ordeal in this last psychiatric unit before leaving the U.S. Regular Army. At one point, I experienced anaphylactic shock of my throat when I was in an elevator. I had to be rushed to the emergency room at the base hospital there at Fort Sam Houston in San Antonio, Texas.

And to think that folks take medicine today like its candy for adults. Why not find a better way? The biggest problem today, I think, is that folks don't have the time. Normal, everyday tasks, work, life with family, friends, entertainment, etc., keep folks so busy that they don't have the time to find a better way.

Believe me: There are better ways to live than living on any Psychotropic medicine. I have proven this in a huge way. It was because of my faith and finding the truth that helped lead me to **My Escape from the Mental Prison of Drugs!**

Psychotropic drugs will alter and change your thinking, keeping you in a virtual "Mind Prison" or "Prison of the Mind"!

I got to know some folks in that unit, and to this day I still have fond memories of them. One person I met was named Lisa (don't recall her last name?). An Army girl, she drew a picture of Ziggy for me. And then there was a black man who was helpful throughout my stay; he became the unofficial leader of we"misfits" in the service of this psychiatric unit.

Even in the end, when I was leaving, he took me to the airport to catch the plane back to Syracuse. I really did miss him, and many times throughout the years I have thought of all of them, wondering how life had turned out for them.

There was some Puerto Rican guy who every morning used to exercise with me, so that we would feel normal in beginning of our days there at Brooke Army Medical Center or BAMC for short.

We used to have a Jamaican art therapist who would take us not only to the art room to draw, paint, and make pottery; but she also took us bowling in town at a local bowling alley. She also brought us out to eat at a restaurant.

It was the first time I was off any of the three bases since my breakdown.

They even had a swimming pool for us, and a therapist/ nurse would bring us to it on the base of Fort Sam Houston in San Antonio every week too. She really did the best she could for us with what she had been given to use while we were staying in that hospital. She was truly one of the blessings of my stay there, and when I eventually left I gave her a huge hug and told her how she truly had helped me in this ordeal. We both had tears in our eyes when we let go of each other.

I was utterly amazed how the staff seemed to know exactly where we patients were at any given time. They had cameras everywhere, and the acoustics in that place were amazing.

Probably one of the most difficult times of my stay was the group therapy we had, involving a huge circle of patients, doctors, nurses, and anyone else who was involved in our treatment. It was quite boring of a meeting, which would go on for at least two hours, as we listened to everyone's issues. Many times, I almost fell asleep while waiting my turn to speak about what was bothering me.

In one way, though, it was somewhat therapeutic, as it was good to know that you were not alone in your struggles, nor that your situation was as bad as others. There's always someone else who is worse off than yourself. Remember this in your own life.

CHAPTER 62

I really was looking forward to going home when I was in that unit. And yet it felt safe, because it was familiar to us all. Realizing that I would on my way home soon, after going through three hospitals, two states, and a period of three and a half months since my nervous breakdown, was scary. I felt like I would get too attached to being there when I got out.

But that day I left the base and Army for good, I was wondering just what life would be like now. I had so many questions.

What made it difficult was the acclimatization process back to the civilian world. There was a stigma among veterans (including myself) with "mental issues" who feared being viewed by others as "second- class citizens."

I wrote about this stigma in an article and submitted it up in Maine, where I lived when I was married the first time. They actually printed it in the *Bangor Daily News.*

To this day my own family (not all of them, but many of them) still believe I am "crazy." I assure you, I am not crazy! Honestly, I believe that I am more normal than most of the folks around me.

I recall being nervous on the plane as I flew back to New York from Oklahoma. I have restarted my life over six times.

One of the greatest advantages I had was the support from family and friends, especially my incredible and wonderful mother, Angela Marie. I tried sleeping most of the way on the plane. The problem was that my thoughts were racing about the next stage of my life. Of course, I made a huge to do list. This is a habit I have had since I was young.

I recall the moment of meeting my mother at the Syracuse airport. Running into her arms and giving her a big hug and kiss was so very comforting. I felt like staying in her arms forever. Tears flowed freely. Our neighbor Jean Tarbona came along. She later married my cousin John Logan.

It really was good to be home, and finally out of the U.S. Army. I was in a total of one year and one day. The ordeal would take me twenty-eight years of therapy to process.

Some months later, the rest of my belongings were returned from the Military (from my last Army unit). They were delivered right in front of the last house I lived at with my mother, before I moved out in 1992.

CHAPTER 63

What I went through all those years I would not wish on anybody. It literally took away in some small sense "my feeling like a man," What helps a man to identify himself is his work, his career. That was totally taken away from me, and no doubt caused me some serious mental suffering over the years.

Even though it's been thirty-two years, I still feel cheated by what happened to me. I lost the beginning of my adulthood, and I never totally recovered from this experience. And while I do get compensated (for which I am truly thankful) for what happened to me, I'd rather have been able to live my life normally, like so many of those I knew growing up.

Of course, nobody could tell you exactly what "normal" is in this society. It's sort of like the law: The law is what the judge says it is. When thinking about that statement, I always think of part of the verse in the Holy Bible that says, "where no law is there is no Transgression…"

A person can overcome getting physically hurt, and possibly be fairly normal. But when something affects you mentally, it can affect your entire life, and it can affect everything you ever do or everyone you become involved with for the remainder of your days.

Mental issues can be dealt with and overcome. Most of us who have had such dramatic, traumatic experiences may never fully recover, making life difficult, despite any and all good that might happen. It's literally like being in a prison in one's mind.

For me, this prison of my mind from the so-called "medicine" was not helping at all in the long run. It was more like a band-aid, and something that did not get to the very root of the issue. As a Christian believer, the root of the issue is "sin." Isn't this truly the "issue" of everything wrong in our lives and world? I'd say a resounding Yes!

CHAPTER 64

I was really glad to be home! I was more than thrilled to be eating a home-cooked meal. But I also was somewhat apprehensive about my future.

My mother had become the driving inspiration in my life. She was reason I had such drive in my own life. She helped me on the road to recovery and get me back on my own two feet for the next six years, at which time I would buy a seventy-foot mobile home in the same park where my Uncle Richard lived.

He had lived in one of the mobile home park's forty trailers for over three decades.

Eventually, my mother would live in this park as well, for about four years before she died, leaving us behind. My nephew lived in her mobile home during her last few days on this Earth, and then, after my mother died, my sister Melissa inherited the home.

It was a long road to recovery, but when you have that mindset to accomplish a goal, you can do it! This is definitely the power of your mind.

I would have loved to see the look on the face of every

single doctor I ever had, every last psychiatrist who had treated me, when I told him or her I was drug free. For me, it felt like something had been lifted off my body and that a light literally went on in my mind. Sort of like switching on a light bulb is what it felt like in my brain!

It would be a feeling of true victory. In the last seventy-plus years on the entire East Coast of the United States, I am one of the only veterans to have ever gone from taking ten Psychotropic drugs daily to being drug free; and to this day, over thirteen years later, I am still free of drugs!

Looking back on my path to becoming whole is somewhat of a blur, because so much has happened. I had at least twelve jobs in that period of time. The side effects of those drugs made it very difficult to keep a job, and so I quit my jobs.

The best salary I ever had working was probably in the military, which honestly wasn't more than around $18,000 a year! Thankfully, I am doing well now.

CHAPTER 65

I recall the day when I picked up my sister's first born, my nephew Dana, to take him somewhere in my car.

After a minute he had asked, "Hey, Uncle Michael, how are you making all these green lights, and not catching any red lights?"

I told him that the medicine, along with some good music and my mind, would start working like a computer. I knew exactly how much pressure to apply on the gas pedal to make each green light. I never got a red light during a three-month period. How many folks could say that they could drive for three months straight without having to stop at a red light? Other than myself, I had never met anyone who could say this!

My real goal at that moment was to deal with a problem I was having with my kidneys. The VA actually discharged me so that they would not have to pay for the surgery.

My mother helped me get Medicaid to pay for my surgery. My doctor, William K., ended up cutting my urethra and attaching it back, because there was a blockage there. Amazingly, ten years later I ended up with kidney stones due to the scar tissue of that surgery. It was a very difficult operation, both of: the cut urethra and the kidney stones. Both involved having to go under the knife. I never liked the idea of surgery, let alone the actual surgery itself.

After that operation was over and I was healed, I needed to find a job. The first job I had ever had was at a grocery store. Thankfully, Peter's IGA, where I had worked when I was sixteen, took me back. I was probably one of the better workers that company had ever had, but this second time I got caught for stealing. Not something I am proud of at all.

I got caught at the bottle return for putting in more bottles that I had taken in and pocketing the cash myself. The stupid thing was that we're talking less than $2.00. I got fired over taking $1.87.

I was young and acting juvenile. This was the only time I ever stole from a job, and it was stupid and embarrassing, since the police escorted me out.

Thankfully, no charges were pressed, and I was simply fired. Also, this was the first and last time I was ever fired from a job. I quit all the other jobs I ever had except the U.S. Army, from which I was discharged.

Frankly, looking back on my working life, I always was a very hard worker. The way I see the way many folks work today, I am glad to have left the workforce years ago. Many folks I see in stores are just lazy, not wanting to do the work. They care more about their lives outside of work. Most folks seem to know very little about the products being sold or what their supposed to do in their job?

Even now, decades later, folks who own their own business' tell me how difficult it is to find a good worker nowadays.

Some of my jobs in the civilian world were:

1. Grocery. Peter's IGA in Syracuse, New York, for two years' total, two different times. I am the only person in the history of Peter's IGA (was family owned five store company) who one day the aisle I was working on was completely filled—the dog and cat food aisle—which had no back stock. Even one man who worked over forty years said he was never able to do such an incredible feat. I did it in three-and-a-half months. The Hardest Worker Award I received in eighth grade helped to propel my life in accomplishing such feats.

2. Wegmans grocery store on Pond Street in Syracuse. At this company's first store in Syracuse, I cleaned the meat market. There I worked with a few real nice Christian guys: Ernie Overend(who worked for Wegmans for over thirty-three years. In 2018 he decided to get another job. I graduated with him. His sister Beth also still works there); and some other man whose name I cannot recall (he was also an Italian and a Christian man). Growing up, and even to this day, Ernie Overend and his sister Beth are two of the nicest, most genuine people I have ever met!

3. Syracuse County Public Library in New York. I was a page: putting away books, shelf reading to see books were where they should have been placed,

and running errands for my boss, Librarian Karen Pitoniak. In 2017, I finally called her and told her about my first published book "My Poetic Blessings," which I submitted for that particular library known as "Central" in downtown Syracuse. I decided to send her a copy and autograph it for her. She was thrilled to get it and said she enjoyed reading it.

4. Restaurants: The Holiday Inn, which is now Crowne Plaza near downtown Syracuse. I was a dishwasher. I was learning to be a first cook. Too stressful, but interesting. One-time famous singer Conway Twitty ate chicken wings there while I was working. I ended up cleaning his plate and getting a copy of the check he signed. The Clam Bar. I worked as a prep cook. Working in a restaurant was one of my favorites! I am a full-blooded Italian, and being in the kitchen comes naturally. I also worked in the biggest kitchen at Syracuse University.

5. I also worked some temporary jobs. One temp job was setting up tents for a country fair. My photo made the front page of the newspaper's "Life" section. I also put together a "Deb" store in what used to be called the Syracuse Carousel Mall (it's now called The DestiNY Mall).

CHAPTER 66

One of my all-time favorite jobs was working for Syracuse University. I first was a janitor for the Hall of Languages. Then I worked in the Big SU Bookstore as a Cashier for one day. The rest of the time at the Bookstore I was stocking notebooks in 1988. I am proud to say that my poetry book, *My Poetic Blessings*, was sold in that very bookstore. In 2018 while visiting Syracuse, however, I found that they were downsizing their library, getting rid of the poetry section — and my book.

My last job at the university was as a dishwasher in the largest dining hall on campus, called the Schine Student Center. I was second in command of the dishes, pots, and pans. I really enjoyed working with the people at this job, and every year I visit Syracuse I stop by and see some of those I knew then and who still work there.

While working as a dishwasher at the Schine Student Center I would eat my lunch most days in the cafeteria. The 1988 Syracuse University Basketball Team would always sit at the same table I ate my lunch. I got the opportunity to sit with players Sherman Douglas, Derrick Coleman and Rony Seikaly who all went on to play Professional

Basketball after college!

It was a crazy job that involved being on your toes and working as fast as you could. But every job is important, no matter where you work.

I worked with one worker, Charlie, for a week.

He's Lebanese who with his parents owns King David's, a restaurant on the Syracuse University campus. His brother owns "King David's II" up in Fayetteville, New York, where I grew up. Every time I walk in his place to say hello, he's always working, but that's because his restaurant is always busy.

He always offers me free food, and half the time I refuse and thank him anyway. Sometimes I take the food and thank him afterward. He won't even take a tip from me. For the past seventeen years, I always stop by his restaurant whenever I visit Syracuse on my annual trip.

CHAPTER 67

I also had a job at the Syracuse County Public Library, which I enjoyed. I was a page, as the term goes. I put away books, shelf read the bookshelves to see that they are in order, and cleaned up tables and chairs to see that they were presentable for the patrons. I also ran errands for the staff.

I finally made it as a "page" (pun intended) in the library, which was a goal of mine. And now, years later, I am in libraries with my own book, *My Poetic Blessings*. In 2017, I submitted two of my poetry books to the Syracuse Public Library. There are a few poems that aren't mine at all, but I enjoy and I simply wanted to include. It is sold on *www.Amazon.com* currently, with 130 pages for $6.03.

In 2016 I had Amazon CreateSpace publish *My Poetic Blessings*. I plan to do the same with this writing.

As I said before, I had several jobs up until 1991, when I was in the psychiatric ward at the Syracuse VA Hospital. I was in that ward at least sixteen times before never returning there again and becoming drug free.

It was the same year that, finally, after five years of

trying, I finally got my VA Disability Check. If you ask most veterans , they will tell you that the process used to take years. You feel like you're forever in limbo while waiting for your compensation from the government. It took five long years to get that check.

Waiting was the hard part!

To many, this may sound like such a great place in life to be. But honestly, I would have rather had a career than having to deal with what happened to me. So many times, people I have known used to say that I was so lucky not to work.

How is what happened to me a lucky thing?

In reality, some of the most famous and most intelligent folks who have ever lived experienced some mental issues. Some examples include: Actress Patty Duke (Bi-Polar Disorder), Artist Walt Disney, Artist Vincent Van Gogh (Depression), President Abraham Lincoln (Depression), Composer Ludwig van Beethoven, Four-time Super Bowl Champion Pittsburgh Steeler Quarterback Terry Bradshaw (Depression), Winston Churchill, Author Charles Dickens, Writer Ernest Hemingway, Artist Extraordinaire Michelangelo, Sir Issac Newton, etc.

CHAPTER 68

Well, as I said previously, I have worked in many jobs. And, sadly, I wasn't able to keep any of those jobs due to the side effects of the drugs I was taking. There came a point where I accepted that I would be retired and no longer working (it's so important to remember the old saying: "God, grant me the serenity to accept the things I cannot change, courage to change the things I can, and wisdom to know the difference").

I have written stories, poems, one song (which became a title track on an album by Christian contemporary singer Twila Paris called "True North"), and created art that I have either had published or given away.

When I was in high school, I submitted two poems that were printed in two of the four yearbooks between 1981 and 1985 at my senior high school Anthony A. Henninger in Syracuse.

I also wrote a short story called "The Dream Before My Race" which was printed and published in a small magazine called *Syracuse Seasons* in Syracuse by Bryan Wilbur who was Editor and Owner of the magazine. Eventually those magazines were sold to the Library of Congress; the Library of Ireland (in the country of Ireland); and the Syracuse County Public Library in downtown Syracuse.

I have also written two children's stories that currently have not been printed or published, but are on the back burner and which one day I hope to finish and publish also.

I have created several works of art over the years since I was a little boy growing up in Fayetteville. My precious mother supported me in my pursuit of my artwork, realizing that I enjoyed this creative outlet. I have given some of my art away and kept some myself. Some of my art went inside my poetry book. I get in periods (moods) where I may produce much art or none at all.

CHAPTER 69

Since I was twelve, I have been waiting to fall in love once and for all with a woman. I have dated a few women in this area. One of them was Charlene B., who is now married. I have no idea what her new last name is. She was at least twelve years older than me.

Charlene had been married twice before and was a Catholic. Her being Catholic was part of the reason it wouldn't work out.

Another woman I dated for four months was named Robin W. She was a registered nurse who retired from Valley View Nursing Home. She was around eighteen years older than me. I still see her every now and then walking in areas where I am driving.

There was another RN, Janette, whom I dated only one night (I wanted to date her more). She used to work for the Blair County Jail in Hollidaysburg, Pennsylvania. I couldn't reach her after the first date, but then saw her again working as a cashier some years later for Martin's Food.

CHAPTER 70

I encountered another strange woman named Millie, who I met once at Chris' Yard Sale Store on 17th Street, in Altoona. I had spoken to her on the phone a few times, and then she sent me a photo of her because I had forgotten what she looked like.

I really wasn't interested and told her this.

Honestly, more than once I had to tell her I wasn't interested. How many times do you have to tell a woman NO before she gets the picture?

She began on a weekly basis to tell the store owner, Chris, that she liked me. To this day when I go in the store to buy movies, Chris will tell me she still asks about me. Finally, several months later she stopped.

This woman reminded us both of a stalker, and Chris once said to me, "Wow, Mike, I hope I don't hear about you on the news one day!"

"What do you mean?" I asked.

"I mean I hope I don't hear that she has shot you because she knocks on your door and says, 'If I can't have you, then nobody can!' kind of statement to you and then shoots you dead!"

We both had a good laugh.

"No, man, that won't happen," I reassure him.

One day upon entering Chris' Store he says, "I've got something' for you!" and then proceeds to hand me a card from Millie that is in an envelope with the word "Michael" on the front and some flower drawn next to it.

What I tried to write about here was simply a part of my life story that I wanted to write, so that at least the events of what happened to me in the U.S. Army would be accurately interpreted. This way, family and friends one day when I am gone will have the truth about my life as I lived it. It's not exhaustive though!

No doubt even after this book is published I will have forgotten something.

I was not going to be a victim of the VA Medical System like so many men and women I have known and now know. Frankly, I think it is a very sad society in which folks in VA hospitals are walking around like zombies.

But these zombies are everywhere, not just in VA hospitals. Psychotropic drugs alter the way the mind thinks and feels. I would guess that in America today a majority of folks (even truly educated ones) are quite ignorant of the truth about how these psychiatric drugs are keeping folks from their true potential in life. I see it as a slight form of mind control.

I knew and prayed to my Lord Jesus Christ that when I became free from the control of these drugs that I would help others in this life to also break free! Sort of like when Harriet Tubman (a runaway slave back in the 1850s) helped to free slaves. She actually helped free over 400 slaves. The Scriptures tell us that the truth will make us free!

"And ye shall know the truth, and the truth shall make you free."

(John 8:32 KJV)

"For he that is called in the Lord, being a servant, is the Lord's freeman: likewise, also he that is called, being free, is Christ's servant."

(1 Corinthians 7:22 KJV)

I have helped some folks break free from drugs, but many I could not help because they've chosen not to be free. We all have free will in this life, and many choose to remain like the status quo!

Many times, I believe life will turn out one way (because we tried to plan it?), and it turns out a very different, unexpected way.

What happened to me in the military completely and totally changed me and the life I thought that I wanted! Was it better or worse? I will never truly know.

I think we expect our life to turn out the way we WANT it to turn out, and when it doesn't, those **Great Expectations** we may have had in our mind as a young person will soon disappoint us.

The way in which I was able to BREAK FREE from the drugs I was on from the VA Hospital was through an anacronym I learned while living in Maine. The eight letter word is NEWSTART which means the following:

N= Nutrition. You must eat well in order to truly heal yourself. Organic food. Whole Grains, Fruits, Veggies, Nuts, Seeds are the best categories. I also eat Grass fed beef, Wild Seafood, Pasture raised eggs and Free range Chicken.

E= Exercise. Cardio, Stretching and Strength training

W=Water. My philosophy is 5 to Stay alive; 8 to Feel Great and 10 to Rejuvenate! Each glass is 8 oz. The Body is made up of around 70% Water.

S=Sunshine. It's best to get at least 5 to 15 minutes of it daily. I don't use sunscreen unless it's something I buy in the Health Store that I can trust.

T=Trust Christ Jesus as your Savior by Simply Believing that Christ died for your sins, was buried, and Rose again the Third Day!

A= Air. Get outside. Use an Air Filter in your home.

R= Rest, sleep. I try to sleep at least 6 to 8 hours daily. I recently bought a bed called,

T= Time in the Word of God, the King James Holy Bible and anything that's Positive!

This is also my entire Philosophy on Good Health which is also mentioned at the end of this book.

CHAPTER 71

I can say one thing about myself and my life: My mother, grandmother, and Uncle Richard helped to truly raise me and shape my life. I have been told by many women over the years (including recently) that I turned out to be a very kind, generous, loving, and RARE gentleman.

Why, you might ask? Well, a female friend of mine, Jennifer H., who worked at KNY Family Fitness, the local gym I go to (she was there over three years), once gave me the answer as to why she believed I turned out to become the truly sensitive, good man that I have become.

After speaking with and listening to me, she believes that I think more like a woman than a man. I believe this statement is accurate to some degree.

Men in general don't think about other people's feelings. I simply happen to think more with my heart than my head. (Mark my words: I am a straight, heterosexual man.) It doesn't stand to reason that I don't think at all like a man because, obviously, I do. But for some reason unknown to myself, I am frankly a very sensitive man who's very understanding of other people's feelings.

I could tear up simply listening to someone sing a patriotic song, and I cry during some movies or even movie trailers. That is definitely more sensitive than most men and even some women.

Actually, thanks to my parents and my genetic makeup, I have the best of both worlds: the bold, energetic side of my mother, and the slower, rational, and thoughtful side of my father.

For me, Helping others to see the truth is one of my life's greatest joys. Joy is an anacronym for: Jesus, Others, You.

"Let nothing be done through strife or vainglory; but in lowliness of mind let each esteem other better than themselves."

(Philippians 2:3)

"Look not every man on his own things, but every man also on the things of others."

(Philippians 2:4)

One thing you can very quickly learn in the Holy Scriptures is that our Savior, Jesus Christ, and the Apostle Paul were other-oriented men. In this world, there are and have been millions upon millions of people who have lived upon the Earth.

The God of the Holy Bible (King James Version, which I believe that has no errors) is someone who thought of others. He paid the highest sacrifice: The life of His son, Jesus Christ. God the Son had ultimately given the greatest sacrifice: He lay down his very life for His own creation!

Talk about thinking of others. That's truly the most unselfish thought one could ever have in this life. There was one woman in my life for whom I would have laid down my life: my first ex-wife, Maria Dee Roberts.

I have waited half a century to sacrifice my life for a woman whom I would love, and who would be the LAST woman in my life. Every woman I ever truly cared about in this life, and even loved: I truly did sacrifice my life to some degree. There have been five main women whom I have loved in almost fifty years:

1. Theresa Troiano (four months during the summer of 1981, when I was thirteen and a half years old)

2. Patty Warner (age fourteen to sixteen)

3. Cristy Brown (age sixteen to seventeen)

4. Maria Dee Roberts (first wife, age twenty-six to thirty- one)

5. Nancy Raia (age forty-seven to almost forty-eight)

The reason I did not mention ex-wife #2 is because I really didn't love her the way I would have wanted, because she failed to allow me to love her in that way! Also, she turned out to be a phony and simply wanted my money and NOT my love.

I could say that there was a woman I dated for two weeks to whom I would give honorable mention as someone I truly hoped would have turned into a True Love: Charlene. She was living on Morningside Drive in Altoona when I ran into her in the produce department at Giant Eagle Supermarket back in 2012, and she still looked good for being a dozen years older than me. She said she finally had found the "one" in Husband #3. She had been married for three years at the time. She seemed really happy, and I was happy for her too!

Of course, the greatest woman I actually ever loved out of them all was my mother, Angela Marie (Donatis) Manzi. She not only loved me back, but better than ever woman ever could or probably would have in my lifetime!

Obviously, a mother's Love is the greatest love anyone can receive! Certainly, a mother's love isn't the love I am looking for, as I already enjoyed my Marvelous Mother Angela's Love! I speak, of course, of romantic, fairy-tale love.

CHAPTER 72

I was married twice, unfortunately. I only truly loved my first wife, Maria Dee Roberts. Her last name is now Michaels. I think it's sort of neat that her last name is close to my first name. I met her in an interesting way. I was walking in downtown Syracuse one day, telling others the Gospel of Jesus Christ.

The last man that day that I ended up giving the Gospel to was Gary Ingison, who led me to my first wife. You see, upon meeting Gary, he gave me to a list of Grace Believers around the country. I called some in the state, including my good friend and brother in Christ, Norman Hartramph.

I have spoken to Norman via phone since 1990. I have personally met him twice. Norman introduced me to the Uncle Larry of my first ex-wife. Larry ended up introducing me to his niece, Maria, and gave me her physical address. I began to write snail mail letters (of considerable length) to Maria for many months before she gave me her landline phone number.

I began calling my future first ex-wife on the phone for a good year before she drove down from Ellsworth, Maine, to where I lived at the time, in Lyndon Mobile Home Park near Dewitt, New York.

Upon meeting Maria Dee Roberts at that time, I was already in love with her. Within a month or less after meeting her for the first time, I married her. I was not sure about her daughter, though. Right away after meeting my then-future stepdaughter, I knew it would real difficult to deal with her, and I called it off.

My heart broke, and I had trouble eating, sleeping, and simply existing, because I was so in love! I really felt I would die if I did not marry her: my heart ached that much!

So, my first impression was right, but I married her and lived with her and her daughter Jaimie Lee. The next four years were long and difficult, but even with the pain of ups and downs, I would have done it all again!

The story of my first marriage to Maria Dee could be a novella within itself, because of the ordeal in which I went through. So much truly happened in those four years that a three-hour movie could be made out of it all.

We got married at the church she was attending in Ellsworth, Maine, and lived in her nearby apartment. The day of the wedding (attended by nobody in my family, even though everyone was invited) was nerve-wracking, busy, and amazingly beautiful all at the same time.

Sadly, even to this day, when I have mentioned how awful I felt that nobody on my side came to my wedding, there is argument. I have been told and scolded that I invited them (my relatives) on a day that they could not have come. But this is nonsense, because they all knew in advance about my wedding day and could have made arrangements. Besides, I was first among my siblings to get married. I think my father's boss would understand that his son was getting married and he would have given him the day off. Even Maria's first ex-husband was there.

The members of Ellsworth Baptist Church (I had once helped put a whole roof on the parsonage's house) gave in the money envelopes all the money we needed for our honeymoon. The Honeymoon Cabin we rented cost $105, which is exactly the amount of money we received. Not only did they give us money, but they made us a huge meal, with everyone bringing something for the dinner.

Before going to our honeymoon, I drove Maria's mother, Delores, all the way back to Dexter, Maine, from Ellsworth, Maine, which took almost one and a half hours. There used to be a shoe called "Dexter shoes," which they made on her street in Dexter, Maine.

Then we headed to our honeymoon along the coast, where we stayed in a cabin alongside a lake.

Well, we stayed in Maria's apartment for a few weeks until we could find something else. We ended up in several rentals until we decided to buy a home of our own in Bucksport, Maine.

Ellsworth, Lamoine Beach, Surry, Orland, Brewer, and Bangor were where we had rented apartments. It was culture shock after living in a big city like Syracuse. Then there was the adjustment of living with a wife and a stepdaughter.

It would have been easier to have first lived with Maria and start our own family, but that was wishful thinking.

There were aspects about Jaimie that I really liked, but I knew no matter how long I was married to her mother that Jaimie Lee would probably never change her thoughts of the man who broke up the union between she and her mother.

As Actor Jack Nicholson said in One Flew Over the Cuckoo's Nest, "Well, at least I tried damnit, I tried! Nobody could say that I didn't!" It may not be the exact words, but it's close!

CHAPTER 73

Maria got pregnant during our honeymoon. I was now twenty-eight years old and wanted a family that I could call my own. My father, Dominick Samuel Melice, was around the same age when my mother became pregnant with me. My brother Christopher was thirty when his wife, Mary, became pregnant with their daughter, my niece Marisa.

Sadly, within five weeks of being pregnant, Maria had a miscarriage. The entire event was one of the most traumatic events in my life, and almost proved to be fatal for Maria.

It was at night that this shocking and disturbing experience rocked my world, and I thought I was going to lose the woman I had loved to pregnancy. I was woken by Maria, who was on the bathroom floor, making sounds. Right away I went to her, picking her up and yelling, "Are you alright?! Maria, are you okay?"

She mumbled somewhat incoherently as I struggled to lift her up. I could see in the toilet she had lost the baby and a lot of blood. Finally, she had enough strength to get up. She kept saying, "The baby, the baby, he's in the toilet! We can't leave the baby!"

Now, I had never in my life had any incident even remotely close to what I was up against, and my heart was beating quite fast. I simply wanted to get her and what was left of our five-week-old baby fetus to the hospital immediately. I yelled to her daughter, Jaimie Lee, that we had to get her mom to the hospital right away.

At the time, we lived in Ellsworth, Maine. This should have been a quick, in-the-car-and-go trip. But her daughter, famous for arguing with me, wanted to take the dog, Ladie. I told her, "No, Jaimie, we need to leave ASAP. Your mom lost a lot of blood! I don't want her to die!" Finally, Maria told her to get the dog and let's go.

I was speeding down the road, really wanting to have been there minutes ago. Thankfully, we got her to the emergency room soon enough, and she was taken care of right away. During this time, we found out that she was allergic to Demerol. Her ex-husband, Carl, was notified, and he came down to wait with us.

I was glad that he was around to wait with Jaimie. Carl had adopted Jaimie when Maria went to him for help when she was just a baby.

Carl was very knowledgeable about living in rural Maine. He built his own home, had retired from a paper mill, once had twenty-six milking cows, and at his age of sixty-five, the man had been able to do just about anything.

He was quite the outdoor type, who could have lived in a Louis L'Amour novel (I had read many of Louis L'Amour novels, thanks to second ex-wife's mother Dorothy!). A real Daniel Boone type of man who was a Christian, wanting to lead Maria to the Lord.

Their marriage only had lasted six months, and it was more like a father-daughter type of relationship than anything. Carl wanted to help save her soul and life. He was a good man who treated me as I tried to treat him: like a gentleman! He was twenty-five years older than Maria, and thirty-four years older than me.

As much as I loved Maria, dealing with Jaimie Lee was very difficult a job. When I had met Jaimie Lee, she had fourteen parakeets and some fish. By the time the marriage was over, she had two dogs, one cat, six parakeets, several fish, an iguana (from her Uncle Maria's brother that thankfully did not live long), several chickens, and a horse. She wanted to be a veterinarian.

She instead became a photographer, wife, and mother of three boys, last I heard. I even once called her and spoke to her. After twenty years she still was bitter about the whole ordeal. I tried to speak to her as one believer to another believer, but she wasn't mature enough to simply speak to me for the short time I wanted to speak with her.

I was hoping it would be a peaceful conversation, thinking she'd have matured by now, but she was talking pretty much like the spoiled, angry, bitter child I had known back in the nineties.

There are many things I could say in this story about being married to Maria, but I want to say that I truly loved her more than any woman since or after her. And that I did try to treat her in a loving, respectful, caring way as any Christian husband should treat his Christian wife!

I even loved Jaimie Lee no matter how awful she had been toward me or treated me. I had always tried to walk in love toward her, but she sadly, simply, did NOT want her mother married to me. I found years later that Carl (her first ex) died at the age of eighty- two, and his house and land went to Jaimie. I only hope that she and her mom are happy now.

CHAPTER 74

The house we eventually bought a year after getting married was a lovely home in a great location in Bucksport, Maine. The day that I went to see the house on Bucksmills Road was Valentine's Day 1996. What I did not know was that there were hearts on the wallpaper in the entrance way and living room of the house.

A dirt-and-stone driveway led to the house, located on four acres with a small orchard on the left. The home was custom made with two bedrooms, a small living room, a small kitchen, a small bathroom, a small den, a basement, and a root cellar, and a loft bedroom on the second floor. The fact that you could walk out onto the roof from the loft was very neat.

It had beautiful wooden floors and ceilings. Two acres of woods edged the back of the house, facing north. There was a small garage workshop (it needed much tender loving care) to the northeast and a chicken coop next to the garage/workshop. We grew vegetables in the garden, on the east side of the property. Maria had a flower garden, too.

The property was situated in the most perfect way for

any home out in the country. The previous owners, Richard and Sally Small (with whom I still speak), had put a ton of money into creating this home, so that even the water from rain or snow had great drainage.

There was a sweet spring behind the house, with a huge rock slab over it.

There was a period of time when we were separated a few months, and I was living in Bangor in a town house and also an apartment in Bucksport. My most memorable time in that town house is one afternoon when Maria came by to see me (Jaimie was in school at Bangor Baptist Academy, where I one time had met recording artist Paula Dunn and her husband, whom Maria and Jaimie had known).

We also went to see a Christian concert at the auditorium at Bangor Baptist Church, featuring one of my all-time favorite Christian contemporary artists, Twila Paris. The group "Avalon" opened for her.

At the end of the concert, I waited in line to meet Avalon and Twila Paris. Maria and Jaimie didn't want to meet them. I had given Twila a song of mine that I had copyrighted but gave her permission in writing to use called "Going Northbound." She used it, adding music and more lyrics and making it her title track on her album "True North."

I was driving a Honda Spree going north from Syracuse to a community college (Onondaga Community College) when I got the inspiration and words for this song!

One afternoon, Maria came by while Jaimie was at school and we made love in the living room of the town house I was renting. It had been a long time since that had happened between us, and that is what made it so special.

There were times in this first marriage where weeks went by between our lovemaking. If you ever want to make a man go crazy, all a wife has to do is take away affection and intimacy, and it won't be long before you have a very frustrated, resentful, and angry husband on your hands.

The Holy Bible talks about this separation for a time, but only with the consent of both man and wife.

"Let the husband render unto the wife due benevolence: and likewise, also the wife unto the husband."

(1 Corinthians 7:3)

"The wife hath not power of her own body, but the husband: and likewise also the husband hath not power of his own body, but the wife."

(1 Corinthians 7:4)

"Defraud ye not one the other, except it be with consent for a time, that ye may give yourselves to fasting and prayer; and come together again, that Satan tempt you not for your incontinency."

(1 Corinthians 7:5)

Physical touch is very important for everyone. Myself, I love hugs. They are a real stress relief that costs nothing but a moment of time.

Another big event that occurred during my first marriage was meeting local famous billionaire author Stephen King. I had read some of his books, and really enjoyed his writing, though I had never bothered to read many of his writings because they seemed very warped.

He happened to be signing one of his many books at the

Book Marc, on February 9, 1999, and I just so happened to be walking past. As soon as I saw the line outside the door of this Bangor bookstore (he lived only a few blocks away), I knew that he was there. I had waited a whole ten years to meet him so I could give him the Gospel of Jesus Christ.

I had told a fellow named Craig at a Syracuse VA Group Therapy that I was going to one day meet Stephen King and make sure he knew the Good News of the Gospel, by which a soul is saved from going to Hell and the Lake of Fire.

I somewhat nervously walked into the bookstore and asked where the poetry books happened to be located. Thankfully, they were literally right next to where King was sitting. O Lucky Day! I sat down next to him as he was signing and speaking to these many hordes of fans who had lined up waiting to get him to autograph his new book.

I began to say a quick heartfelt prayer of how I would give him this Gospel. Just the next moment, a female fan came up to the table and started to jump up and down in a very excited fashion, proclaiming, "Stephen, Stephen! O, Stephen!" Here was the moment I had been waiting for more than a decade. I stood up and I shouted to the woman (looking right at her), "Please, Miss, he's a man, just as I am a man!"

I proceeded in telling her the Gospel and then turned to Stephen King and said, extending my hand to shake his, "Hello, Stephen. I've been waiting over a decade to tell you this. Jesus Christ, who was God the Son, died for your sins, was buried, and rose again.

Simply believing this Good News will save your soul, Stephen! I surely hope that you believe this wonderful scripture found in the King James Holy Bible, 1 Corinthians 15: verses 3 and 4."

He smiled and simply said, "Well, thank you," as he continued to shake my hand, looking at me with a big grin. He is one of the most famous people to whom I ever gave the Gospel.

On November 19, 1999, when I was walking in downtown Bangor, en route to the Coin Shop not far from the Book Marc bookstore, a small, four-door Subaru struck my left leg and I ended flying up in the air, coming down on wobbling feet, and hitting my head on the windshield. Downtown Bangor's Main Street starts out as a rotary with two lanes. I had gotten hit about 120 feet from the start of the rotary, and was around 5 to 7 feet from the curb when I got hit. I was told later that I broke the windshield with my head! I was about to sell a photo of Abraham Lincoln, which I had found in the basement of the Hier Avenue house in Syracuse where I grew up.

Now, if anyone has ever gotten hit by a car, you will realize a few things that happen:

1. Time moves in slow motion in your mind. You know how they show this in the movies, when someone gets hit. Well, in real life this most definitely happens in your mind. That two seconds felt more like ten seconds in my mind.

2. Your life really does flash through your mind, recalling all the monumental moments that occurred in your life. But they go in and out of your mind very quickly.

3. Because of the shock and adrenaline after getting hit by a car, you will say to yourself, "Did I really just get hit? No way! You HAVE to be kidding!" Your Mind really cannot believe you were just hit by a car.

After being rushed to Eastern Maine Medical Center, I was taken into surgery to deal with my leg. Believe me, the pain was some of the worst I have experienced (I watch real close when I cross streets now).

Amazingly, I could not find a lawyer in that town who would take my case. You see, I wasn't in the crosswalk when I walked across that street, which was a rotary that had started near where I was crossing. In Maine, if you're not in the crosswalk and you get hit, it's your fault because you're breaking the law.

Interestingly enough, author Stephen King had also gotten hit by a vehicle the same year (1999) as I got hit. The man who hit him actually went out of his mind and died one year later on Stephen King's birthday. Stephen's wife bought the truck and compacted it into the size of a cube is what I had heard from my lawyer. My divorce attorney, Mr. Norton of Bangor, was also one of his lawyers on his legal team.

What really sucked was that I was told in the beginning of this trauma that I may never walk again, and that scared the heck out of me. But with will and determination, I recovered faster than most, because your mind is one of the greatest weapons you own.

Remember the children's book, *The Little Engine that Could*? I THINK I CAN, I THINK I CAN!

My Grandma Gugliano used to always say to me, "It's all in your Head!" She was definitely ahead of her time with this thought!!

The last thing I will say about my first marriage is the following: In the end, Maria simply wanted her belongings and $1,800 dollars. She wasn't greedy. She even gave me a poem ("One Day at a Time"), which I placed into my first book, "My Poetic Blessings." She did live in the house for quite some time (I cannot recall exactly how long), and I had to live in a rental down the road right in the town of Bucksport.

Honestly, I loved Maria and would have hoped that the marriage worked out. She remarried a few years later and wrote a book called " *In Gratitude of Grace*", just two years before I had my first book published. Her daughter, Jaimie, got married and has three children and a mini farm in Patten, Maine, which belonged to her adopted father, Carl Boutaugh.

CHAPTER 75

The second woman I was married to was the largest mistake I have ever made. Her name is Kathy M., from Huntingdon, Pennsylvania. Everyone called her "Kate," including myself. I could say in all honesty that I loved her dog, Mattie-girl, who was a sweet, 15- pound Jack Russell. She wasn't the normal jumpy Jack Russell, though at times she did that when she wanted to go out; but typically she was pretty calm.

I was the only man I knew whom she let near her and in her lap. No other man could do that! Even Mattie-girl knew I was a good man. Dogs, I believe, can sense these things.

Kate's daughter was a decent woman who seemed to have it together. She was married and had three boys. I was at the hospital when boy #3 was born. I cannot recall his first name, but his middle name is my first name. I always wondered if they would explain that to him?

I've tried to wipe out the memory of the second ex and her family, since she made life a living hell in the divorce.

She had a son whom we took in the last year and a half

that I was married to her. For much of that time, we enjoyed fishing, hunting deer, and hunting ginseng together.

I had never hunted anything before, and the experience itself was interesting and fun. I enjoy being in nature, but hunting isn't my cup of tea. While fishing once down at Lake Raystown, not far from the Spillway Kate, Jim (her son) and I saved three folks after their car had rolled and flipped into the water.

The story made the newspaper in Huntingdon, Pennsylvania, that week.

Besides, having grown up in a big city, you won't find many, if anyone, my age who ever hunted in the woods. Fishing, maybe.

I think one of the greatest things in the world that gives my life joy: is Giving to Others!

"It is more blessed to give than to receive."

(Acts 20:35c)

I have been called "rare" by several women in my lifetime because of how I treated them. What I never understood is the whole concept of cheating on your girlfriend or spouse. I never cheated on anyone I was married to or dated. I was always loyal!

CHAPTER 76

I can say that, despite the fact that the one goal that I wanted to attain in this life was to find and love a woman, that I am proud to have accomplished something equally amazing.

In the years following my conversion of becoming a Christian, a Grace Believer, I have had the pleasure and opportunity to have given the Gospel of our Salvation to over 15,000 folks.

Some famous folks I had given the gospel to are: Stephen King; TV evangelist with a super church Joel Olsteen (he could not tell me himself); rock band Judas Priest; an actor from the TV show *The Jeffersons*; and several well-known Pennsylvania politicians including Congressman Bill Shuster; Senator Jubelirer; Senator Robert Santorum; Representative Richard Geist; and Senator Arlen Spector.

Whether it is telling the truth about the Holy Bible, health and nutrition, or the U.S. government, giving the truth about anything and everything I possibly could is by far one of my greatest achievements of my life.

Life is short, and the truth is by far the most Important

aspect in this life. Without the truth, life is but a total lie and difficult to figure out. What I have told you in this book about myself is the truth, the whole truth, and nothing but the truth! So help me God!

CHAPTER 77

When I left Maine, I didn't want to move back to my hometown of Syracuse. My father's side was from Pennsylvania, so I decided to move there. Though I ended up on the opposite side of the state from where he came from. Folks would call it the Pittsburgh side and not the Philadelphia side.

I got in touch with Tracy Plessinger, a Pastor of an assembly in Altoona called at the time Ambassador Bible Church. (They had another group up the mountain called Grace Alive Church of Mountaindale. A few years back they opened up their Altoona assembly in a Greenwood storefront not far from where I first lived in the area.)

A man named Mark and his family from the local church that I attended took me in when I moved to Pennsylvania.

I moved to Altoona on September 4, 2000. That day, the gas price was 99 cents a gallon.

Mark and his family were so very accommodating to me. They were genuine, kindhearted, and wonderful Christian people whom I have been very blessed to have known the past eighteen-plus years. I still keep in touch with Mark and his family.

Life here in Altoona over the past eighteen-plus years has been very interesting, to say the least. Upon moving here, I was to move into a place called Elizabeth Apartments (which currently is getting refurbished as I write this). The second day I was here, Mark and another brother from the church, Bob Beam, helped me unload the U-Haul into the apartment.

After three days of having my belongings at Elizabeth Apartments, I went back with Mark to let the owners it wasn't a place for me. My reasons:

1. They never told me that I would pay a separate gas bill. I thought it was included in rent.

2. The electric company said that there had not been an electric meter for my apartment in 11 months.

3. The bedroom window opened up to the center of the building, showing bricks.

I almost didn't get my deposit back, but the owner kept my first month's rent due to my signing a one-year lease. Gratefully at least I did get the deposit back though legally they didn't have to give it back.

I went to Saylor Rentals to store my stuff in a storage unit, and then took a few weeks to find a place on Union Avenue. Ken Bickel was my first landlord at 609 Pottsgrove

Road. He owns K & C Dentures on Valley View Boulvevard in Greenwood, Pennsylvania. I was on the second floor of a duplex. Below me were two twin sisters who worked together at some local department store called Value City, which no longer exists here. The furniture store Value City does, but the department store went out of business years ago.

I had lived there about three years when I moved to 2705 Union Avenue, which was the home of Rona Eardley. Rona, my Landlady, had a little miniature collie dog and was in her seventies. She also was a Christian and was sort of like a grandmother to me the three and a half years that I lived above her home (another duplex).

She kept telling me that I could connect my TV to her cable wire, which came up into my apartment from her home below. I finally tried it, but a few days later told her I disconnected it. When I moved out of her place to the next town over, in Hollidaysburg Manor Apartments, she tried to keep my deposit.

I was stunned, really, to think she would have ever done that, since she was mostly very kind to me, and I was very good to her. But I got all but $20 back from her after calling the cable company and telling them what she had done.

One day, when I had been living at 59 Clover Drive in Hollidaysburg for a little over a year, she knocked on my door.

"Here," she said quickly, handing me a check and walking away.

I met a woman there named Robin Way, a nurse whom

I dated for about four months. She went to live with her mother in Eldorado Mobile Home Park in Altoona to assist with her ailing health. Robin had retired a few years after she moved in with her mother and is currently still living there with her mother.

I currently live in an 1889 Victorian apartment house on the corner of Tenth Street and Lexington Avenue. I have lived there since June 25, 2011. It is owned by Kathie Phelps, who, coincidently, was my therapist before I moved here. I think I had seen her as a therapist at least four years. She offered a huge discount on my rent the first three years of my stay here. She knew my financial situation after my second divorce and was very kind to me during that time and since.

In the eighteen years I have been here, I attended Grace Alive Church of Altoona for almost ten years. I left that assembly four times.

The first time I left Tracy Plessinger's assembly was because, after mowing the grass up at the Mountaindale Conference Center (the church's second group), I had asked Treasurer David for $5 gas money. Instead of giving me any cash, he said I could have whatever coins I found in the grass. Imagine how upset I was to have seen Tracy and Dave Greenwood have a good laugh over this. It took another two years before I went back.

The second time I left was because two women accused me that I was trying to come onto them. I simply was speaking to them, and they judged my INNOCENT intentions to be otherwise?! It was another two years before

I went back again.

I don't recall what the third reason was as to why I left, but I left the fourth and last time because of the way they were treating my good friends Mark, Debbie, and their daughters. I left the church in 2012 shortly after Mark and Debbie had left, never to return again.

The ways in which I am keeping busy is that I am also writing a second poetry/art book and a children's story. I finally became debt free in 2017, after paying off my 2013 Subaru Outback. I go to the gym daily and keep busy in my life. I also created a bumper sticker and a poster for restrooms. I have sold over a hundred of each item. Strangely, my poster has been stolen at least twenty-five times in both Altoona and Hollidaysburg.

Some things I have learned in my short fifty years of my life are:

1. Having the right attitude is key to many problems in life.

2. You have to live your life, not someone else's. You can give the right advice to someone, but they have to choose what they will do with your advice.

3. Food really does affect your health, for good or bad, depending on what you stick in your mouth.

4. Exercise is important to good health. Weight training, cardio, and Stretching are the essential three elements you need, I believe, for good health.

5. You also need to supplement your diet with a good multi- vitamin and multi-mineral. You also need fatty acids, probiotics, enzymes, etc. We cannot get the proper nutrients that we need from our soil, which is depleted on a huge scale.

6. Without knowing the Lord Jesus Christ as Savior in your life, you do not have a chance for not going to hell! Christ died for your sins, was buried, and rose again the third day: Believing this Gospel is what saves a soul.

7. Water is essential to life. Without the proper type and amount of water, you will die a slow death that may be painful both in body, soul, and spirit.

8. Deep breathing and shedding tears are good in helping eliminate acid burden and toxins. Infra-red saunas and steam rooms are also good for eliminating toxins from your body!

9. Don't expect good results without sacrificial work! Learning to give to others is one of life's greatest joys! Live to give, not live to take (in 2014 I coined the phrase of my philosophy "Live to Give").

10. Teaching children the right way to live is a parents' greatest gift to society's burdens.

11. Frankly, I don't think that getting involved as a "Light" in politics serves the greater good, due to a system of corrupt politicians who don't want the greater good. They only wish to fill their own

pockets with fiat money and have more power.

12. Time in God's Holy King James Bible will always benefit a person who knows the Lord Jesus Christ personally as their Savior. Redeeming the time in His Word not only benefits the individual, but those around him or her, because the days are evil in this present evil world.

13. Live and Let live is one of life's greatest principles. My mother would say, "To each his own."

14. You're more rewarded in this life and the next for serving Jesus Christ than you would be for serving money, which is corruptible and not lasting. Loving money is the root of all evil.

15. Proper education is the key to a safer, healthier, and more productive society.

16. Real wealth is good health.

17. The mind of Christ is key to your success.

18. Without your health, your money has no value and is meaningless to you. Just look around at those who are wealthy but cannot enjoy it due to their bad health.

19. Listening to someone is one of the greatest gifts you can give to them.

20. Loving someone takes real work and effort. To say it doesn't take work to love someone is being truly being ignorant.

21. Ignorance is one of man's greatest downfalls.

22. Proper rest and sleep, I believe, are essential

elements to optimal health.

23. Laughter is one of life's greatest medicines.

24. Being debt free is one of the greatest freedoms we can possess in America.

25. People are more important than possessions.

26. Never rely on others to get something done, is what I have found. If you want something done, do it yourself.

27. If you plan on planning your life, stop. I tried that (and though you need some plan and goals for your life) and learned it won't happen the way you would like. Nothing ever happens the way you would like it to.

28. Realize that you are only human. Quitters never win, and winners never quit. Only try your best. I learned this in fourth grade.

29. Truth is stranger than fiction. Knowing in society what is the truth has become difficult thanks to a media in America that was bought in the beginning to give us in this country only the news that the powers-that-be want to give to us. There is what truly happened (the truth), and then what the media reports (the created truth many times. Not the whole truth!). Of course, God has the absolute truth in His King James Holy Bible.

30. Helping others to believe the truth is not your job. Giving others the truth that you believe is